50 WALKS IN

Herefordshire
& Worcestershire

50 WALKS OF 2–10 MILES

First published 2003
Researched, written and updated 2009
by Nick Reynolds

Commissioning Editor: Sandy Draper
Senior Editors: Penny Fowler
  and David Popey
Designer: Tracey Butler
Picture Research: Vivien Little
Proofreader: Pamela Stagg
Cartography provided by the Mapping
Services Department of AA Publishing

Produced by AA Publishing
© AA Media Limited 2009

Published by AA Publishing (a trading
name of AA Media Limited, whose
registered office is Fanum House, Basing
View, Basingstoke, Hampshire RG21 4EA;
registered number 06112600)

Enabled by [Ordnance Survey] This product includes
mapping data licensed
from the Ordnance Survey® with the
permission of the Controller of Her
Majesty's Stationery Office. © Crown
Copyright 2009. All rights reserved.
Licence number 100021153.

A03628

ISBN: 978-0-7495-6298-4
ISBN: 978-0-7495-6323-3

A CIP catalogue record for this book is
available from the British Library.

The contents of this book are believed
correct at the time of printing.
Nevertheless, the publishers cannot be held
responsible for any errors or omissions or
for changes in the details given in this book
or for the consequences of a[ny reliance on]
the information it provides. T[his does not]
affect your statutory rights. V[e have tried]
to ensure accuracy in this bo[ok, but things]
do change and we would be [grateful if]
readers would advise us of a[ny inaccuracies]
they may encounter.

We have taken all reasonable [steps to]
ensure that these walks are s[afe and]
achievable by walkers with a [reasonable level]
of fitness. However, all outdoc[r activities]
involve a degree of risk and th[e publishers]
accept no responsibility for a[ny injuries]
caused to readers whilst follo[wing these]
walks. For more advice on wa[lking safely]
see page 144. The mileage ran[ge shown]
on the front cover is for guida[nce only]
– some walks may be less than or exceed
these distances.

Visit AA Publishing at theAA.com/bookshop

Cover reproduction by Keenes
Group, Andover
Printed by Printer Trento Srl, Italy

Acknowledgements
The Automobile Association wishes to
thank the following photographers and
organisations for their assistance in the
preparation of this book.

Abbreviations for the picture credits are as
follows – (AA) AA World Travel Library

3 AA/C Jones; 9 AA/C Jones; 28/29 AA/C
Jones; 58/59 AA/C Jones; 80/81 AA/C Jones;
100/101 AA/C Jones; 116/117 AA/C Jones;
128/129 AA/C Jones; 138/139 AA/C Jones;

Illustrations by Andrew Hutchinson

Every effort has been made to trace the
copyright holders, and we apologise in
advance for any accidental errors. We
would be happy to apply the corrections
in the following edition of this publication.

Author acknowledgement:
The following information sources were
invaluable: *Nancy Elliott's Dore Workhouse in
Victorian Times* (1984, Workers' Education
Association, Ewyas Harold Branch) for
Walk 41, and Gerry Calderbank and Martin
Hudson's *Canal, Coal and Tramway* (2000, LC
Promotions) for Walk 26. For their help
the author would also like to thank Richard
Phillips of Badsey (Walk 5); Professor Jean
Emberlin at the National Pollen Research
Unit (Walk 18); David Williams of Golden
Valley Apiaries (Walk 48); John Coleman,
Golden Valley Community Coordinator,
and Christine Hope at the new Longtown
Post Office (Walk 50). Thank you to Pamela,
Eleanor and Fiona for letting me go 'walking
working'. This book is dedicated to my Dad,
who started me walking.

Right: Path through the woods, Walton Hill (Walk 7)

AA

50 WALKS IN
Herefordshire
& Worcestershire

50 WALKS OF 2–10 MILES

Contents

Contents

Rating

Each walk is rated for its relative difficulty compared to the other walks in this book. Walks marked +++ are likely to be shorter and easier with little total ascent. The hardest walks are marked +++.

Walking in Safety

For advice and safety tips see page 144.

Locator Map

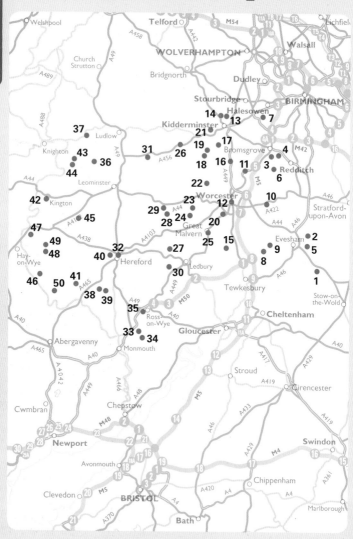

Legend

--→--	Walk Route	░░░	Built-up Area
❶	Route Waypoint	░░░	Woodland Area
– – –	Adjoining Path	🚻	Toilet
＼∖／	Viewpoint	🅿	Car Park
•	Place of Interest	冉	Picnic Area
⌂	Steep Section	)(	Bridge

6

Introducing Herefordshire & Worcestershire

Worcestershire is a county of generally rolling hills, save for the flat and fruity Vale of Evesham in the east and the prominent spine of the Malverns in the west. Nearly all of the land is worked in some way; arable farming predominates – oilseed rape, cereals and potatoes – but there are concentrated areas of specific land uses, such as market gardening and plum growing. The county is not without surprises – in Stourport it has Britain's only town created because of a new canal; it has Droitwich Spa, a former site of inland salt production; and its long distance footpath, the Worcestershire Way, has some fine 'ridge' sections, at Rodge Hill (see Walk 22) in particular.

In Herefordshire the land is hillier, abutting in the west with the Black Mountains ridge that defines the border with Wales. Crops are important here, but there are more green fields – for grazing, silage or hay – because this is livestock country. You may be surprised by the large number of sheep, since the 'Hereford' breed of cattle has acquired such fame. And you can't walk for long in this county without seeing an apple orchard.

There are short walks around each county's capital. In the city of Worcester (see Walk 12), which is by far the larger of the two, parts of the core have been reasonably well held on to, New Street, in particular, and Worcester's Commandery (museum) is a regular crowd-puller. The city of Hereford (see Walks 32 and 40) essentially escaped wartime bombing but suffered considerable damage from sorties made by trendy architects in the 1960s (and subsequently), but the cathedral area and the riverside – Castle Green and Bishop's Meadow – have retained, thus far, their charm.

The two counties offer plenty of other 'things to do'. Highlights include some time on a river, the view from Hereford Cathedral's tower, watching a horse working the cider mill at Shortwood Farm (near Pencombe), and eating too many plums in the Vale of Evesham.

In these pages you will find much evidence of past activity: there are churches, castles and mansions (some in use, some in ruins), railways (disappearing and disappeared), canals (extant and extinct) and a pot-pourri of personalities. No conscious effort has been made to select routes beside rivers, yet there are several. Perhaps they hold a subliminal attraction, or is it just that their abundance makes them hard to avoid? They include the rivers Severn, Wye, Avon, Teme

> ## PUBLIC TRANSPORT
>
> The three linear walks in this book are Walks 21, 25 and 40, using train, train and bus, respectively. (It's always better to take your car to the end and use public transport back to the beginning.) Of the other 47 there are frankly few where you could reach the start by public transport if, say, staying here on holiday. The urban centres are the focus of bus service provision; for a village to have a bus service may mean no more than a bus into town on market day morning, returning in the afternoon.

and Frome, to name just five, while in Herefordshire's Golden Valley (see Walks 41 and 48/49), the river is called 'Dore', a name that possibly arises from a confusion of languages. The Welsh referred to the valley's river as dwr, meaning 'water', and some think that the Normans mistook this for d'or, the French for 'of gold' – if this is the case, it was an appropriate mistake to make! If it is coastal walking you want, then you've come to the wrong place, but otherwise you're sure to find something to delight you in Worcestershire and Herefordshire.

Using this book

Information panels

An information panel for each walk shows its relative difficulty (see page 5), the distance and total amount of ascent. An indication of the gradients you will encounter is shown by the rating ▲ ▲ ▲ (no steep slopes) to ▲ ▲ ▲ (several very steep slopes).

Maps

There are 30 maps, covering 40 of the walks. Some walks have a suggested option in the same area. The information panel for these walks will tell you how much extra walking is involved. On short-cut suggestions the panel will tell you the total distance if you set out from the start of the main walk. Where an option returns to the same point on the main walk, just the distance of the loop is given. Where an option leaves the main walk at one point and returns to it at another, then the distance shown is for the whole walk. The minimum time suggested is for reasonably fit walkers and doesn't allow for stops. Each walk has a suggested map.

Start Points

The start of each walk is given as a six-figure grid reference prefixed by two letters indicating which 100km square of the National Grid it refers to. You'll find more information on grid references on most Ordnance Survey maps.

Dogs

We have tried to give dog owners useful advice about how dog friendly each walk is. Please respect other countryside users. Keep your dog under control, especially around livestock, and obey local bylaws and other dog control notices.

Car Parking

Many of the car parks suggested are public, but occasionally you may find you have to park on the roadside or in a lay-by. Please be considerate when you leave your car, ensuring that access roads or gates are not blocked and that other vehicles can pass safely.

Right: Path towards North Hill, Malvern Hills (Walk 25)

William Morris's Broadway

*A haunt of the Arts and Crafts pioneer towers
above this Worcestershire village.*

DISTANCE 5 miles (8km)   **MINIMUM TIME** 2hrs 30min

ASCENT/GRADIENT 755ft (230m) ▲▲▲   **LEVEL OF DIFFICULTY** +++

PATHS Pasture, rough, tree-root path, pavements, 9 stiles

LANDSCAPE Flat vale rising to escarpment

SUGGESTED MAP OS Explorer OL45 The Cotswolds

START/FINISH Grid reference: SP 095374

DOG FRIENDLINESS Sheep-grazing country (some cattle and horses too)
so only off lead in empty fields; some stiles may be tricky

PARKING Pay-and-display, short stay, 4hrs maximum in Church Close, Broadway;
longer stay options well-signposted

PUBLIC TOILETS Church Close car park, country park and Fish Hill Picnic Place

---

If Caspar Wistar were alive today, a springtime visit to Broadway would give him much pleasure. Visitors come in swarms to this Worcestershire village, which lies against the edge of the Cotswolds – understandably, for it's one of the sweetest places in England. They buzz around a linear honeycomb, the honey-stone buildings stretching for the best part of a mile (1.6km). Horse chestnut trees flame with pinky-red candelabras and walls drip with the brilliant lilac flowers of wisteria. Caspar, the 18th-century American anatomist after whom the wisteria genus was named, would surely not miss this photo opportunity. (The fact that wisteria and pink horse chestnut are not 'authentic', as both were introduced to Britain centuries after Broadway's older buildings were constructed, doesn't seem to matter!) There are many buildings of note in Broadway, not least the partly 14th-century Lygon (pronounced 'Liggon') Arms. The Savoy Group bought it for £4.7 million in 1986. History has contributed to this price – in 1651 Oliver Cromwell stayed there on the night before the decisive clash in the Civil War, the Battle of Worcester.

Arts and Crafts

Less historic but more affordable is Broadway Tower. The 6th Earl of Coventry's four-storey folly (1799) has served as home to a printing press and a farmhouse, but is best known as a country retreat for William Morris (1834–96). Appropriately, in 1877 he founded the Society for the Protection of Ancient Buildings. Artistically, Morris empathised with the Pre-Raphaelite Brotherhood, a group, primarily of painters, founded in 1849 by William Holman Hunt. They believed that British art had taken a 'wrong turn' under the influence of Raphael, who, with Michelangelo and Leonardo da Vinci had made up the trio of most famous Renaissance artists. The English Pre-Raphaelites challenged the teachings of the establishment, producing vividly coloured paintings, lit unconventionally, which had an almost flat appearance.

BROADWAY

In 1859, Morris married Jane, an 18-year-old model for Dante Gabriel Rossetti, his British-born mentor. Rossetti's wife had committed suicide and Rossetti later had an affair with Jane. Morris and some friends (including Rossetti!) set up a company producing crafted textile and stained-glass products. Morris was fascinated by pre-industrial techniques. Disillusioned by the Industrial Revolution, he was attracted to Socialism in the 1870s. He joined the Social Democratic Federation and became increasingly militant writing extensively on Socialism and lecturing. All the while he was writing prose and poetry and, when Tennyson died in 1892, Morris was invited to succeed him as poet laureate. He declined and died four years later.

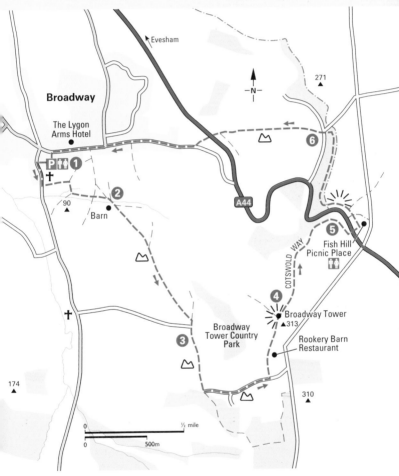

WALK 1 DIRECTIONS

❶ Walk back down Church Close then turn left. At the far end of the church wall turn left, soon passing a tiny, narrow orchard. Go through a gate before a strip of grass and turn immediately right to reach a simple stone bridge over a rivulet. Turn half left, across uneven pasture. Go to the right-hand field corner and pass through a kissing gate. In 35yds (32m) cross over a stile to reach a bridge of two railway sleepers beside a stone barn.

2 Cross this to a waymarker through a boggy patch to two stiles. Maintain the line to another stile. Cross a large field to a stile, then continue in this direction following footpath signs across three more fields. In the third field go through the gate on the right side and cross a tree-lined track to a gate 62yds (57m) ahead.

3 Slant uphill, passing in front of a stone bungalow. Just before the woodland ahead turn left. Join a tarmac road, steadily uphill. At the brow turn left over a stile, into Broadway Tower Country Park, and pass the Rookery Barn Restaurant. A tall kissing gate gives access to Broadway Tower.

4 Beyond the tower go through a similar gate, then take the little gate immediately on the right. Move down, left, 22yds (20m) to walk in a hollow, through pasture and scrubby hawthorns, to a gate in a dry-stone wall. In 93yds (85m) meet a tractor track. Turn left and in 37yds (34m) go right by the Cotswold Way acorn marker. Walk parallel to the track in a similar hollow, aiming for some bright metal gates among trees. Beyond these go straight ahead and in 45yds (41m), at the next marker, bear right, walking above the road.

5 Pass the first footpath sign leading to the road and follow

the Cotswolds Way signs as the road bears right. Join a tarmac track parallel to the road past Broadway Quarry and soon meet the road. Cross it using the central refuge and reach Fish Hill Picnic Place. Continue to follow the Cotswold Way signs to the left, and up some steps to a trig point with good views. Follow the Limestone Trail signs ahead, entering a wood with a fence to the left. At the next signpost bear left down into a hollow and up the other side. At the top bear right, following a footpath sign, and leaving the Limestone Way. Follow this narrow path (beware many exposed tree roots) near the top of this dense wood. Eventually take steps on the left down to cross a road junction.

6 Go over a stile to take the field path signposted 'Broadway'. Descend sweetly through pastures and over another stile. Swing left then right to pass over a stile, under the new road, emerging near the top end of the old one. Turn right, on to the dead end of Broadway's main street. In the centre, 60yds (55m) beyond two red telephone boxes, turn left, through Cotswold Court arcade, to Church Close car park.

A Fruity Route Along Cleeve Hill

A low, wooded ridge looks over a rich, fertile plain where the popular Victoria plum is grown in abundance.

DISTANCE 4.5 miles (7.2km)   MINIMUM TIME 2hrs

ASCENT/GRADIENT 225ft (69m) ▲▲▲   LEVEL OF DIFFICULTY ✦✦✦

PATHS Paths across fields, stony tracks and village roads, 5 stiles

LANDSCAPE Level farmland with distant hills

SUGGESTED MAP OS Explorer 205 Stratford-upon-Avon & Evesham

START/FINISH Grid reference: SP 077469

DOG FRIENDLINESS On lead near sheep; some freedom in arable fields

PARKING Outside Littleton Village Hall on School Lane, Middle Littleton, or village street (tithe barn parking for visitors only)

PUBLIC TOILETS None en route

The Vale of Evesham, renowned for its fruit, is virtually flat, but the growers who farm the land are constantly of the opinion that the economic 'field' on which they 'play', slopes against them. The most frequently cited objection is that producers abroad get (more) governmental assistance, facilitating a large supply of cheaper imported fruit, which consumers are willing to accept.

Plums with such evocative names as Pershore Purple and Pershore Yellow Egg used to dominate the region, but nowadays the Victoria accounts for three-quarters of the commercially grown plums. The plum is the first tree to come into flower in spring, showing its delicate white petals even before the sloe (blackthorn).

According to folklore, plums may, apparently, be used to make a love potion. In my experience, however, they are vastly more effective as a laxative than as an aphrodisiac!

Tunnel Vision

One of the ways in which cherry growers have made themselves more competitive is to grow the fruit on dwarfing rootstocks; as the name suggests, this means that the tree does not grow to any great height, making the labour-costly task of picking the fruit much easier. A further benefit is that the smaller trees can be covered by a plastic tunnel. Although there are now several types of plastic tunnel, in England the so-called 'French tunnel' has been around, coincidentally, since roughly the time that the Channel Tunnel began to be drilled. Such a substantial investment is best thought of as an insurance policy, protecting the fruit from summer rainstorms.

There is considerable potential to be realised from combining these two simple technologies. Perhaps other trees, such as peaches, almonds, apricots and figs, will be grown in tunnels if suitable dwarf rootstocks can be cultivated.

CLEEVE HILL

Shaping the Future

Although growers are anxious to have soft fruits such as strawberries available early in the season, it is also an advantage to be able to prolong the season. This is achieved by taking plants out of the ground during the shortest days of December and January, then arresting their growth by keeping them in cold storage (which of course incurs a cost) until required, not planting out the last until August.

On our behalf, supermarket buyers make the assumption that we will only eat perfectly proportioned strawberries. Hives of honey bees are routinely used to maximise levels of pollination (see Walk 48). Two separate studies have suggested that honey bees also reduce the percentage of misshapen fruit from about 30 per cent to below 5 per cent... presumably, as you read this, somebody is trying to work out why!

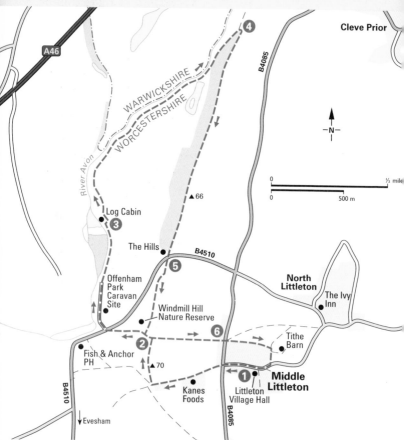

WALK 2 DIRECTIONS

❶ Walk westwards up School Lane to the B4085, here called Cleeve Road. Cross diagonally left to take a rutted, stony track, screened by a hedgerow from Kanes Foods. At a junction of tracks turn right to pass beside a gate, then another, following a blue arrow. After 350yds (320m), you reach an opening on the right and a line of plum trees making a field boundary; on the left is a metal gate.

❷ Go through this gate, entering Worcestershire Wildlife Trust's Windmill Hill Nature Reserve. Descend steeply, ignoring crossing tracks, to another stile and across one field to the B4510. Follow the signposted 'Cleeve Prior' footpath through Offenham Park caravan site. (Keep on the road for 220yds/201m for the Fish & Anchor.) Take a stile out of the caravan park to walk on a stone track beside the river.

WHERE TO EAT AND DRINK

Rather early on in the walk, and just a couple of minutes off the route, is the Fish & Anchor, which welcomes both dogs and children. South Littleton has a post office stores and a fish and chip shop, open Wednesdays to Saturdays at lunchtimes and Mondays to Saturdays from 5pm. In North Littleton, The Ivy Inn serves hot food and cask ales. You may sit outside beside a green. It also has some children's play equipment and a skittle alley.

❸ At a log cabin move to the right to take a double-stiled footbridge and resume your riverside stroll. Continue through mostly ungated pastures for over 0.75 mile (1.2km). Through a small gate, leave the river by taking the right-hand fork. Ascend through trees to a clearing and a path junction.

❹ Turn sharply right, back on yourself, soon walking into trees again, to follow a popular (and sometimes muddy) bridleway. In

a shade under 1 mile (1.6km) the B4510 cuts through the hill, beside The Hills. Cross over and move right to a fingerpost, but follow the path for just 75yds (69m).

WHAT TO LOOK OUT FOR

As you walk through the caravan site you may notice that the caravans are raised, standing on breeze-block pillars about 3ft (1m) high. This flood protection measure reduces the risk of damage by flooding, but by no means removes it.

❺ Go through the gate into the nature reserve here, and follow the waymarked, contouring path, giving fine views over to the west. After 440yds (402m) you will recognise your outward route. Turn left here, up the bank, retracing your steps for just 30yds (27m), to Point **❷**. Once at the top go straight across, walking with the line of plum trees on your left-hand side. When this ends, maintain this direction until you reach the B4085.

❻ Cross the road and go straight ahead. From the second field you will see the tithe barn. Before some young trees take a kissing gate to the right. In 15yds (14m) turn left to visit the tithe barn, or keep ahead to reach the village road. Turn right again, shortly to reach your car at the start of the walk.

WHILE YOU'RE THERE

In the 1970s the Middle Littleton Tithe Barn, once used for tithe payments to the Abbey of Evesham (see Walk 5), was lovingly restored. It's open from 2pm to 5pm (April to October), so time your walk so as not to miss it. Documents show that the barn was in use in about 1370, but carbon dating puts its construction nearly 100 years earlier. Eleven magnificent bays span its 136ft (41m) length – that's about two cricket wickets – and the apex of its roof is over 40ft (12m) above its stone-slabbed floor.

The Ups and Downs of Tardebigge Flight

*Visit Worcestershire's famous big wet steps,
steeped in economic history.*

DISTANCE 5.5 miles (8.8km)   MINIMUM TIME 2hrs 30min

ASCENT/GRADIENT 295ft (90m) ▲▲▲   LEVEL OF DIFFICULTY +++

PATHS Tow path, pastures, field paths and minor lanes, 14 stiles

LANDSCAPE Generally rolling rural scenery, and a whole lot of locks

SUGGESTED MAP OS Explorer 204 Worcester & Droitwich Spa

START/FINISH Grid reference: SO 974682

DOG FRIENDLINESS Off-lead on tow path, under control in fields, lots of stiles

PARKING Limited space, so park tightly and considerately, on north and east side of road bridge

PUBLIC TOILETS None en route

In some respects the British are a nation of slow learners: how often do we hear of a large construction project for which the final bill was vastly in excess of the original projected cost? The canal builders of the 19th century were often not much better. In 1791 an Act of Parliament gave the go-ahead to build the Worcester and Birmingham Canal, setting aside £180,000. It was only in 1815 – 24 years later – that the route to Worcester was available to commercial traffic, and the sum that had been spent was a whopping £610,000. It seems that cost projections were invariably optimistic, rather than realistic. Even at that price, the project had been scaled down, literally, for the plan to take the larger barges that plied the Severn was abandoned.

The Tardebigge Challenge

The Tardebigge Flight was just one of the challenges of constructing the Worcester and Birmingham Canal. The tally of locks along the 16-mile (25.7km) stretch between Tardebigge and Worcester is 56. Add to that five tunnels and several reservoirs, some of which the canal builders were obliged to provide for mill owners along rivers affected by the canal, and it is not only the locks that escalate!

Stoke Prior Salt Works

The Worcester and Birmingham Canal benefited from the discovery of salt at Stoke Prior in 1825 – the salt works were built around the canal shortly after. The works are still clearly visible on the suggested map; note in particular the 'Reservoir (brine)' at grid ref SO 947664. This was the works that John Corbett (see Walk 11) purchased in 1845.

While Corbett must take the credit for the subsequent pre-eminence of his factory there, he must have been assisted by the competition between canal and railway. The Birmingham and Gloucester Railway had opened in 1841, and in 1851 another line followed: the Oxford, Worcester and Wolverhampton Railway.

TARDEBIGGE

Back in 1771, long before the Worcester and Birmingham Canal was conceived, James Brindley had engineered the broad-beamed Droitwich Barge Canal, right into the town's salt production centre. It ran for 5.75 miles (9.2km) to the River Severn, taking salt down and bringing coal up. Perhaps as a response to the railway threat, this 'cul-de-sac' was opened up in 1853 by cutting a mere 1.5 mile (2.4km) long, narrow-beamed channel from the centre of Droitwich to Hanbury Wharf, joining the Droitwich Barge Canal with the Worcester and Birmingham Canal – the so-called Droitwich Junction Canal. Transportation of salt by canal ceased in 1914.

Even if you are not a canal-boat lover, the Tardebigge Flight is a memorable spectacle – it just goes on and on. It has a total of 30 locks within 2 miles (3.2km). There are 17 at the start of the route (if you choose Walk 4) and 13 at the end.

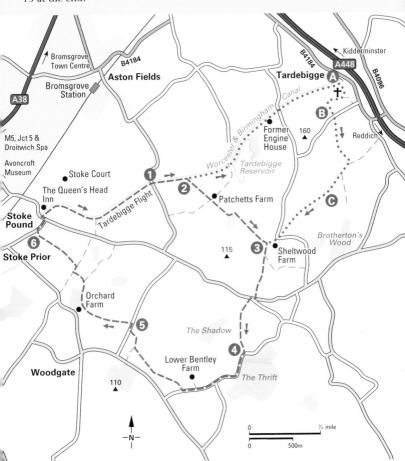

WALK 3 DIRECTIONS

❶ Cross bridge No. 51 and turn left, taking the tow path on the south side of the canal. Follow this to a point about 15yds (14m)

before the next bridge – No. 52. (If you are doing the Walk 4 extension, pick it up here.)

❷ Turn right here, into some trees, then down a field. Cross

17

WHAT TO LOOK OUT FOR

On Walk 4, you'll pass the former engine house (whose life as a pub ended in 2006). In conjunction with the Tardebigge Reservoir, it controlled the lock system's water levels. Repeated wetting and drying takes its toll on the lock gates – they are being constantly replaced. Each has a metal plate showing when and where it was crafted. Which is the newest gate you can see?

WHILE YOU'RE THERE

Conceptually the Avoncroft Museum of Historic Buildings is unique – a collection of historic structures dismantled and reassembled in one place. Perhaps a 'dry' topic, but lots of effort has been put in to making it a family-friendly trip. At Stoke Prior is St Michael's Church. It was here that, in 1901, John Corbett (see Walk 11) was buried.

a double-stiled footbridge among trees then keep straight ahead, over the driveway to Patchetts Farm. At a three-way fingerpost keep ahead (fourth finger missing!) to skirt a copse to the left, then another stile and a two-plank bridge. Cross two more fields, keeping a hedge on your left. You will come to a gate on your left, close to a broken oak tree with a substantial girth. (Walk 4 rejoins here.)

❸ Turn right. Within 110yds (100m), go through the gate ahead (no waymarker), ignoring one to the left. Go a quarter right (or skirt the crops) to find a stile in a wire fence. Retain this diagonal to cross a simple footbridge of three planks, then find a narrow stile in the next field's corner. Walk with the hedge on your left to reach a minor road junction. Turn right for about 55yds (50m). Turn left to cross several undulating fields, passing a pond to your left and swapping field-edge sides at a new metal gate, to reach a minor road.

❹ Turn right. Follow this for 0.5 mile (800m), taking 'Woodgate' at a junction, to Lower Bentley Farm's driveway. Go 140yds (128m) further, to a fingerpost on the right. Cross pasture diagonally to a gap, then to another to the right of a white house. Find a stile

in the bottom right-hand corner of this next field. Go forward for 75yds (69m) then go three-quarters left to a road.

❺ Turn right, and in 75yds (69m) take a handrailed, three-planked footbridge. Cross pastures easily (waymarked) towards Orchard Farm, but then turn right, away from it. Over the corner stile go straight ahead. At a double stile (across a ditch) go half left, and at a gap in the hedge (perhaps with a wooden bar) turn right for 75yds (69m) to two new metal kissing gates. Now turn left, initially with the field-edge on your right, for 650yds (594m), aiming well left of a black-and-white house, for a stile and gate. Soon reach a road.

WHERE TO EAT AND DRINK

Strategically located beside the bridge at Stoke Pound is The Queen's Head Inn, where you can enjoy a canalside beer garden. It has a restaurant as well as a bar menu. Children are welcome.

❻ Turn right. At the T-junction turn left. Join the canal tow path this side of the Stoke Pound Bridge. (The Queen's Head Inn is on the other side.) Now you have over 0.75 mile (1.2km) to return to your car at the road bridge, approximately mid-way up the Tardebigge Flight.

Tardebigge – Seeing the Complete Picture

To view all of the locks of the Tardebigge Flight, see the reservoir and look through the tunnel, take this extension.
See map and information panel for Walk 3

DISTANCE 7.75 miles (12.5km) MINIMUM TIME 3hrs 15min
ASCENT/GRADIENT 380ft (115m) ▲▲▲ LEVEL OF DIFFICULTY ✚✚✚

WALK 4 DIRECTIONS
(Walk 3 option)

Keep on the tow path at Point ❷ and continue to follow it for a little over 1.25miles (2km). At a bend the embankment of the Tardebigge Reservoir looms. Whenever a boat passes through a lock, heading either up or down, a lockful of water is shunted downstream by gravity. Although the locks are not built any wider or longer than is necessary, maintaining an adequate flow of water can be a problem at any time, not just when there is a dry summer. Hence the need for the reservoir, approached from its dammed end.

Beyond the topmost lock of the 30 is another striking feat of engineering – Tardebigge Tunnel, Point ⒶA. Turn right through a kissing gate just before the tunnel, but first descend steps to the tow path to see the light at the tunnel's far portal, 580yds (530m) away. Doubtless some of the extra money went into the making of this tunnel, which was bored through solid rock.

Bear right, up the bank, with the distinctive, Baroque needle spire of St Bartholomew's ahead. The tower was completed in 1777. Cross the gravel car park then walk past the church it serves. Walk with the primary school on your left for just 30yds (27m). Turn left, beside the school and later its playing field, to reach a minor road, Point ⒷB.

Cross the road by a kissing gate and then a stile. Importantly, in the first field strike right of the fingerpost's direction to reach a seen stile. Follow waymarkers across two more fields through gaps and gates. In the fourth field – a shorter distance – go three-quarters right to a stile in a wire fence in an incomplete hedgerow. In the fifth field, walk to another gate, but don't go through it. (It would direct you just right of a two-pole double pylon to conifers.) Move right, to walk with the hedge on your left, eventually reaching a stile and three-plank bridge in the far corner, Point ⒸC. Cross a double stile into the next field. Walk beside field-edges for 700yds (640m) until, at the end of a copse, cross a stile on the right to reach a minor road. Turn left here in the direction of Sheltwood Farm, but in 25yds (23m) go through a gate on the right-hand side. Walk across this field, then go through another gate to rejoin Walk 3 at Point ❸.

Badsey's Wartime Memories

A circuit from Badsey, where German prisoners of war helped feed the nation.

DISTANCE *4.5 miles (7.2km)*   MINIMUM TIME *2hrs*

ASCENT/GRADIENT *80ft (24m)* ▲▲▲   LEVEL OF DIFFICULTY +++

PATHS *Meadow and arable paths, tracks and minor lanes, 23 stiles*

LANDSCAPE *Flat, market gardening and pasture*

SUGGESTED MAP *OS Explorer 205 Stratford-upon-Avon & Evesham*

START/FINISH *Grid reference: SP 070431*

DOG FRIENDLINESS *Can be off lead away from sheep pastures*

PARKING *Roadside parking, Badsey village*

PUBLIC TOILETS *None en route*

WALK 5 DIRECTIONS

Walk south from St James' Church, close to the village stores and post office. Turn left, past The Wheatsheaf Inn and along School Lane, then right into Willersey Road. After 125yds (114m), turn left into Sands Lane. Walk for 500yds (457m), passing Greenacres Animal Rescue, to take a fingerpost, right, opposite wire fence paddocks. Cross a field to a footbridge. Cross the next (small) field diagonally left to find, behind trees, a muddy right-hand field-edge. Follow this to a lane.

This is market gardening country. During the First World War at least 20 locations in Worcestershire were used to house prisoners of war (POWs), as part of the Government's drive to plug the gap left in the farming economy by those who had been sent away to fight. Badsey's POWs were mostly employed by market gardeners – the most labour-intensive of agricultural activities – at a time of low mechanisation.

At the lane turn right, signposted 'Badsey', for nearly 0.5 mile (800m). When this bends right, go straight ahead on a track. After 0.25 mile (400m), at the corner of the last field on the left before houses, find a stile in the hedgerow on the right (or go ahead, then left at the main road, to visit the Sandys Arms). More meadow stiles lead to Wickhamford's memorial hall.

Turn right, passing striking black-and-white houses, some thatched. After 275yds (251m), at a right-hand bend, go left, passing the spectacular Wickhamford Manor, to pass in front of St John the Baptist Church, of weathered sandstone with a squat tower. A

WHAT TO LOOK OUT FOR

Between Wickhamford and Aldington you'll see a long row of water outlets for the intensive market gardening here. Look out for all manner of produce in season – rhubarb, lettuce, spinach, broccoli, beetroot, courgettes, pumpkins and leeks.

footbridge crosses Badsey Brook; follow the left-hand field-edge.

All the market garden produce had to be collected. Basket-making was a specific skill held by some of the POWs, and was particularly welcomed by their new employers. The POWs themselves received 1d of the 4d their employers had to pay to the Government for their services. This became 5d after grumblings were made about these employers having access to preferential rates.

Beside a black wooden shed, join a green-centred track to Badsey Lane. Cross to take a similar track to Badsey Road. Cross this fast road carefully, taking the road through Aldington to a junction in front of The Old Stables. Turn right then almost immediately left. Just after the last house along Chapel Lane, go half right, to a footbridge. Over this, cross one field, then, in a plantation, is the walk's only ascent, far less taxing than the vicious tree stumps on the path itself.

In front of a big dark green shed, turn right. At the B4085 go right for 40yds (37m). Turn right and down this tatty meadow, then swing right through a gap to a footbridge. Veer left a little to a metal kissing gate beside a shed with barbed-wire gates policed by alsatians. A track (green down the middle) leads to Badsey Road. Turn right, then left to view the Manor House on the right.

The Manor House in Badsey was built to house monks from Evesham Abbey who fell sick. A striking black-and-white private residence, parts of it date from about 1350, but it is mostly 16th century. Now flanked by modern, functional houses, it is, architecturally, an oasis. Towards the end of the First World War the Manor House, then a boys' home, was requisitioned to accommodate POWs.

It's debatable how closely a local (and parochial) newspaper reflects the views of its mainstream readership, and so much has changed since that time. Pockets of resentment certainly existed, for example, the 'local rag' gave a dressing-down to a farmer who gave cider to his workers, among whom were German POWs. Hatred there may have been, but perhaps it was more for the war itself than the individuals who had been flung into it unwittingly.

Although some prisoners attempted to escape, such stories are rare. What was the incentive? Despite the mental strain of being a prisoner abroad, and living in what must have been cramped conditions – according to an edition of the *Evesham Journal*, about 100 men were held in the Manor House – to be captured, uninjured, and taken away from the front to do essentially familiar, physical work was a dream ticket when set alongside the hell of trench life.

Continue along this street to the start at St James' Church, where the Manor House's POWs frequently attended services and had their own choir.

Chilled Orange Juice at Hanbury Hall

*A stroll around an estate park, with an opportunity to visit
a rejuvenated country house, its outbuildings and its gardens.*

DISTANCE 4.75 miles (7.7km)   MINIMUM TIME 2hrs 15min

ASCENT/GRADIENT 250ft (76m) ▲▲▲   LEVEL OF DIFFICULTY ✦✦✦

PATHS Meadows, tracks and easy woodland paths, 12 stiles

LANDSCAPE Parkland, woodland, country house

SUGGESTED MAP OS Explorer 204 Worcester & Droitwich Spa

START/FINISH Grid reference: SO 957652

DOG FRIENDLINESS Not good; not allowed in Hanbury Hall's garden
(or house), lots of sheep

PARKING Piper's Hill car park, on B4091 between Stoke Works and Hanbury
(fast road and no sign – easily missed!)

PUBLIC TOILETS None en route

To my mind, the contraceptive pill, the motor car and the television were the three most socially influential inventions of modern times. Further down the list, but a candidate for a top ten position, would come the domestic refrigerator. The commercial exploitation of the refrigeration principle was not realised until 1877, when the world's first refrigerated ship, equipped with a system designed by Frenchman Ferdinand Carré, brought frozen meat to France from Argentina. The now ubiquitous fridge-freezer did not begin mass production until much later, at a General Electric factory in 1939.

Ice Houses

Prior to this refrigeration, the only way of keeping things cold was to use ice. It was stored in ice wells or ice houses. When ice was not available, salting (see Walk 11) was the primary method of preserving meat. Records show that Britain imported ice by ship from Scandinavia right up until 1921, a trade that had begun about 100 years earlier. Before that time it was collected in the winter from any practicable place – ponds, rivers and canals, and even by crushing snow. The ice house at Hanbury Hall is a wonderful specimen. It's a shame that there aren't enough volunteers around to bring it back into use once more.

Built in the mid-18th century, it was sunk 11ft (3.4m) into the ground and topped with a mound of earth. Internally it is 20ft (6m) high and over 15ft (4.6m) across, making it roughly egg-shaped – clever brickwork of which Stephen Ballard (see Walk 27) would have been proud. The dome has a hatch in it (now covered with perspex, providing a useful skylight) and the entrance is a corridor nearly 28ft (8.5m) long. Melted ice drained through a grid in the brick floor.

To some extent it was possible to manufacture ice. Close to the ice house, two deep pools with sluice gates served as reservoirs and, on frosty nights, water would be released into a third, shallow pool, yielding an ice 'crop' to be cut the next morning. Additionally, after heavy snowfalls, all available hands were put to shovels. The snow was compressed using feet, and then flung down the hatch.

Orangery

The Orangery at Hanbury Hall is a wide, nine-bay building, with a lot of glass at the front – sufficient to protect oranges and other frost-sensitive plants from all but the harshest of winters. Architecturally, its highlights are the intricate carvings of fruit and foliage. Built in the 1740s, it was on its own until the 1770s extension to the gardens embraced it. Over the past ten years the gardens at Hanbury Hall have been, not restored, but largely re-created in their original design, using detailed documentation and, when necessary, best guesses.

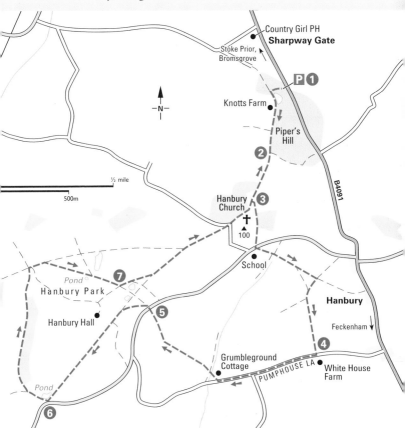

WALK 6 DIRECTIONS

❶ From the bottom of the car park, follow the driveway to Knotts Farm. Go ahead on the left-hand one of two seemingly parallel paths. Keep ahead at a post then, about 350yds (320m) after the farm, reach a gravel track at a fingerpost.

❷ Go straight ahead, with a field boundary on your left. Ascending towards the church, until you reach a stake with two waymarkers.

❸ Fork left, soon passing a spinney, then losing height across a meadow. Take care as the stile and steps here spill you straight on to a minor but fast road. Across this, go beside the school. Cross one field directly then a fraction right, walking diagonally in the third field, 30yds (27m) right of a young fenced oak, to a metal gate. In 70yds (64m) cross a footbridge on the left. Two more stiles lead to Pumphouse Lane.

❹ Turn right. Take a stile and gate on the right just beyond black-and-white Grumbleground Cottage. In 40yds (37m), cross a three-plank footbridge. Follow electricity poles for two fields. Turn right, alongside a wire fence. Reach a road.

WHILE YOU'RE THERE

Hanbury Hall is open from late March until late October, on Sunday, Monday, Tuesday and Wednesday only (plus Good Friday). The gardens open at noon and the house at 1:30pm.

❺ Cross the road to the footpath opposite. At a stile go half left, guided by a wire fence. Pass close to Hanbury Hall's entrance, soon easing away from the perimeter wall to walk 700yds (640m) across parkland, striking a minor road just beyond a picturesque pond on your right. (A line of young trees will be to your left.)

❻ Ignore the minor road, turning immediately right. Hug the boundary fence of the coppice. Continue down the right-hand field-edge. At a junction turn right at a National Trust sign, into this former deer park. After just 60yds (55m), at a small drainage ditch, edge right (blue National Trust arrow). Go straight, to a stile to the left of a clump of fenced

WHERE TO EAT AND DRINK

Country Girl, just 0.25 mile (400m) north of the start at Sharpway Gate, has lunchtime food, including a daily special. Children are welcome. Dogs are restricted to the beer garden. For visitors to Hanbury Hall and/or gardens, the tea room serves soup of the day, jacket potatoes and afternoon cream teas. The cream teas are home-made but, sadly, the chilled orange juice is not.

trees, which hides a round pond. Maintain this line going up the incline – look out for Hanbury church on the left – to reach a tarmac driveway.

WHAT TO LOOK OUT FOR

Some interesting agricultural artefacts adorn the front of Knotts Farm, including a buggy, a butter churn and a cider press. At The White House (adjacent to White House Farm) notice how, despite only being rebuilt in 2000, the boundary walls appears 'old', thanks to the use of mostly reclaimed bricks.

❼ Turn left. When it curves right, go straight ahead to walk in an oak avenue. Keep this line for 700yds (640m), to a minor road. Turn right, then left up to the church. Through the churchyard, find a kissing gate. Shortly rejoin the outward route at Point ❸. Remember to go left, into the woods, at Point ❷.

Breathing Space in the Clent Hills

A brief circuit of the most visited hills in Worcestershire where, in springtime, fields of oilseed rape flood the landscape with colour.

DISTANCE 3.5miles (5.7km)   MINIMUM TIME 2hrs

ASCENT/GRADIENT 660ft (201m) ▲▲▲   LEVEL OF DIFFICULTY +++

PATHS Woodland paths (sometimes muddy), tracks, 5 stiles

LANDSCAPE Mixture of urban cityscape and rolling rural scenery

SUGGESTED MAP OS Explorer 219 Wolverhampton & Dudley

START/FINISH Grid reference: SO 938807

DOG FRIENDLINESS Plenty of running on tops, under control near livestock

PARKING National Trust pay-and-display car park, Nimmings Wood

PUBLIC TOILETS At start

If you are a visitor to Worcestershire then the Clent Hills provide an excellent starting point. More people visit the Clent Hills than Worcester Cathedral. Three car parks provide easy access and make the hills the county's number one non-paying attraction. Of course, proximity to the West Midlands conurbation has much to do with it, but there is something satisfying in standing on the top as dusk falls, watching the city lights begin to sparkle in the distance.

Yellow Spring

Come up to the ridge along the Clent Hills in late April or early May and you may see not only vertical grey blocks of suburban Birmingham, but horizontal yellow blocks of modern rural Worcestershire, created by the flowers of oilseed rape. In 1971 the amount of oilseed rape grown in Britain was a mere 12,500 acres (5,059ha), but it is currently about 1.6 million acres (0.65 million ha). Most is sown in winter. Since it is prone to disease, it is advisable to plant it not more frequently than one year in six. Daffodils aside, it is now the main source of early spring colour in the countryside – Worcestershire and Herefordshire are no exceptions.

Fashionably Sensible

Oilseed rape, a brassica, derives its unfortunate name from the Latin word for turnip, *rapum* (whereas the verb comes from *rapere*, to snatch). Rapeseed oil is just one of many vegetable oils grown for human consumption. If your food has to be fried then it is both fashionable and good advice to cook using rapeseed oil – not only is it without cholesterol (as are all vegetable oils), but of the known vegetable oils, it is the one with the lowest level of saturated fatty acids.

In spite of all this nutritional worthiness, however, only about 65 per cent of the rapeseed oil goes into cooking-oil production, with 22 per cent going to biofuel production; it is used in a number of industrial applications too, such as lubricants.

CLENT HILLS

White Honey

Oilseed rape typically begins to flower in mid-April – earlier than traditional crops – for a 5–6 week period, so beekeepers have to mobilise their bees earlier, to exploit the available nectar (see Walk 48). The nectar sets very quickly, so the beekeeper must extract it from the honeycomb just as the yellow hue is turning to green. Honey derived primarily from oilseed rape is almost white, has a soft texture, and a comparatively bland favour. So much oilseed rape is now grown that it has taken over from white clover as the country's largest source of honey, although some say that white clover produced the best honey (which is not white but pale straw in colour), especially when it grew in long-established, permanent pasture.

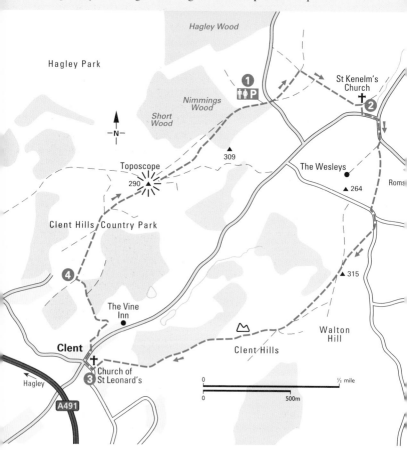

WALK 7 DIRECTIONS

❶ Walk to the car park entrance, turn right and continue for a few paces. Cross the road to a stile and take the left-hand of two options. Immediately you'll see a striking urban panorama. Descend steadily but, at a cylindrical wooden post in the second field, turn right (with a waymarker). Continue across fields, probably populated with horses, until you reach a kissing gate. Here take the forward option (not the right fork), to reach the churchyard of St Kenelm's in the parish of Romsley.

2 Leave by the lychgate. Turn left along the road for a short distance, then right when you reach the T-junction. In about 125yds (114m), take the waymarked path at the driveway to The Wesleys to ascend gently. Move left to find a gate on to a tarmac road. Turn left. Ignore a left turn but, just 30yds (27m) beyond it, take a muddy, gated narrow path into woodland up on the right, angled away from the road and not signposted. Emerge from the trees to the trig point on Walton Hill. Turn left, taking the right-hand of the two options. Follow this for 0.75 mile (1.2km) until a right-hand fork leads to a seen stile out of the trees. Go steeply down two meadows to the road beside the Church of St Leonard's in Clent.

3 Turn right then right again, along Vine Lane. At Church View Cottage, opposite the church's driveway, turn left. (Please follow these woodland directions especially carefully!) In 180yds (165m), take the upper, left fork. In 80yds (73m), at a crossing, go left. After a further 100yds (91m) ignore options to turn right or half right. Proceed for a further 160yds (146m). Ignore the gate and stile on your left to go straight on, ascending steeply up wooden steps. Soon you'll emerge from the trees. Now cross a track then turn right.

4 Keep on this broad, open path, ignoring a right fork, to reach a semi-circular, five-panel toposcope. From this take the initially level path ahead, directly back to the car park.

Overleaf: Nimmings Wood from Walton Hill (Walk 7)

Bracing
Bredon Hill

A walk on Bredon Hill overlooking
Worcestershire's perry country.

DISTANCE 7.5 miles (12.1km) **MINIMUM TIME** 3hrs 45min

ASCENT/GRADIENT 1,115ft (340m) ▲▲▲ **LEVEL OF DIFFICULTY** ✦✦✦

PATHS Tracks, woodland paths, bridleways, minor lanes, 9 stiles

LANDSCAPE Farmland, woodland, panoramic views into Wales

SUGGESTED MAP OS Explorer 190 Malvern Hills & Bredon Hill

START/FINISH Grid reference: SO 953423

DOG FRIENDLINESS Close control needed – cows, horses and lots of sheep

PARKING Roadside parking, Great Comberton village

PUBLIC TOILETS None en route

Bredon Hill is a solitary outcrop of hard, yellowish limestone. The fort on its plateau summit enclosed 22 acres (8.9ha). Today the hill is one of English Nature's National Nature Reserves.

Pershore's Pears

As the name Pershore – 'Pearshore' – suggests, the area around nearby Pershore has long been synonymous with pears (and plums too – see Walk 2). Although perry remains a popular drink, with some manufacturers of perry apparently planting new orchards, many traditional pear orchards have, like apple orchards, been wiped off the map, either for more lucrative forms of agricultural activity, or for house building. An interesting legacy is the presence of pear trees in local hedgerows.

The pear's gene pool is being maintained by setting up a national collection. As many as 120 varieties of perry pear have been recorded; about half of these have been traced in recent years. Specimens have been planted at the Three Counties Showground, near Malvern. In addition, the Worcestershire County Council's Countryside Greenspace Team runs a fruit-tree scheme, like its counterpart in Herefordshire (see Walk 31). Pear, along with other fruit trees such as cherry, apple and plum, is a popular wood for turnery; also, the fine grain of pear wood makes it suitable for engraving when the favoured box wood is not available.

In Worcester (see Walk 12), look out for the city's coat of arms – it bears three black pears. The story goes that when Queen Elizabeth I visited Worcester, the city's 16th-century events manager arranged for a Worcester Black Pear tree to be placed along her route; this pleased Her Majesty, who pronounced that the city's coat of arms ought to display these splendid fruits. Doubtless she didn't actually taste one for the fruit is too tough to eat uncooked, it needs to be served in a pudding such as a crumble, or preserved in syrup. (The same goes for the colour – the fruits are no more black than white grapes are white.) Nevertheless, to encourage some sense of heritage among its children, Worcestershire City Council has provided every one of the city's schools with a Worcester Black Pear tree.

BREDON HILL

Fortified

On the top of Bredon Hill is Parson's Folly. Named after Mr Parson, a resident of nearby Kemerton, it stands on the perimeter earthwork of Kemerton Camp, an Iron Age hill-fort. Elmley Castle's name dates from the 11th century, when Robert le Despenser built a castle on an eastern outlier of Bredon Hill. It was later part of the estate of the Beauchamp family. The castle was again fortified in the 14th century, after interim decay. It is said that stones from this castle were used to build the old Pershore Bridge, adjacent to the present-day A44 road bridge. Today there is precious little to see of the castle itself (on private land).

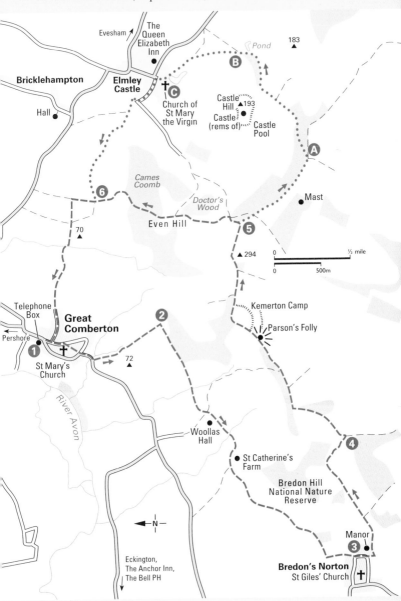

WALK 8

WALK 8 DIRECTIONS

① Begin beside the telephone box in Great Comberton. Follow Church Street. Go through the churchyard; leave by an old iron kissing gate. At the road, go down the '11%' gradient. In the dip find a stile. Ascend two fields (this bit is quite strenuous), with a stream on your left-hand side. In the third field, there is a (wobbly) signpost after 90yds (82m).

② Turn right, initially beside trees. Soon a good farm track strikes across meadow. Ahead is a perfect Malvern Hills view. Follow waymarkers for the next 1.5 miles (2.4km), taking the gravel driveway beside Woollas Hall and skirting St Catherine's Farm. Take a hard track, later tarmac, down into Bredon's Norton. After the first few houses, you reach a junction.

③ Keep ahead for 100yds (91m) to another junction. Turn right if visiting St Giles' Church; otherwise go ahead again, then round a left bend. Go into a field, to the right of two buildings – there's a waymarker on a telegraph pole. Now follow an excellent track steadily upwards,

through several gates, eventually swinging south-east, for at least 0.75 mile (1.2km). Less than 100yds (91m) beyond a single marker post reach a T-junction with 'no right of way' ahead.

④ Turn left, shortly veering right along a field-edge. Ascend for 600yds (549m), then turn right to walk along the wooded escarpment ridge, before an open field leads to Parson's Folly on the edge of Kemerton Camp. Follow the escarpment eastwards, keeping the wall on your left until you reach a small conifer plantation. Just past this, ignore a downward fork, instead following a wire fence for over 0.25mile (400m), to a wood.

⑤ Don't enter the wood; turn left, beside it. Within 150yds (137m), bend right to a junction. Turn left, down a green hollow. At Doctor's Wood veer left to cross an oddly level field, Even Hill (no contours on the map). Find a stile hidden in a dip. Descend steeply through Cames Coomb, along a wide, well-horsed path. Briefly follow a level forestry road, then leave the trees, descending on a track for 400yds (366m) to a metal kissing gate on the right.

⑥ Walk a further 275yds (251m) on the good track to find a path on the left, initially between two hedges. When it ends, go straight ahead. Keep this general line – later a hard track – back into Great Comberton. Turn right to the telephone box.

On to Lovely Elmley Castle

Extend your walk to visit the pretty village of Elmley Castle.
See map and information panel for Walk 8

DISTANCE 9.25miles (14.9km) MINIMUM TIME 4hrs 45min
ASCENT/GRADIENT 1,180ft (360m) ▲▲▲ LEVEL OF DIFFICULTY +++

WALK 9 DIRECTIONS
(Walk 8 option)

Go through the gate at Point ❺.
Walk an easy 0.6 mile (1km) on
a firm, fenced path, flanked by
a steep wooded slope and open
fields. Where the fence kinks
there are gates on the right, and
Wychavon Way indicators. This
is Point Ⓐ.

Go half left, into the woods,
descending steadily on a wide
bridle path. Leave this woodland
for open meadow. Lower down,
veer right, following single
post waymarkers. Cross a
wooden footbridge over a ditch.
Continue descending through
light woodland with bracken. At
a possible fork go left (a wooden
post waymarker soon reassures) to
another footbridge. Here go left,
alongside a wire fence, passing a
long and narrow pond on your
right-hand side.

Within 100yds (91m) of this
pond, reach a new metal gate,
Point Ⓑ. Through this turn left
across a two-plank footbridge. Go
three-quarters right in parkland.
In the next, large field, veer left to
find a stile into a small paddock,
and then another stile. A wooded
path crosses a decorative dammed
pond to reach the churchyard of
St Mary the Virgin in Elmley
Castle, Point Ⓒ.

The chancel of the church was
probably built before AD 1100,
a supposition based in part on the
'herringbone' style of stonework
in the chancel wall. Its font has
a 15th-century octagonal bowl
on a 13th-century square base,
decorated with carved serpents
and dragons. Of particular note
in the church is a set of three
17th-century effigies of the Savage
family, lying down, with four
children kneeling before them.

Through the main church gate,
go forward just 40yds (37m),
then turn left (but you may first
wish to explore the village). Pass
several black-and-white houses,
some of which are thatched. At a
sharp left bend take a fingerpost
to the right, then a little gate,
beside a farm building. Turn left
at the end of this building, using
gates to cross a concreted area;
leave the farm through two more
gates. Follow the right-hand
field-edge. In the third field, after
40yds (37m), turn three-quarters
right at a redundant stile, soon
regaining your line. To the right is
Bricklehampton Hall. Continue
for three fields, crossing stiles and
plank bridges over ditches. Reach
a metal kissing gate to a track
coming down from the left – here
you rejoin Walk 8 at Point ❻.

Huddington Court Terrorists

An easy ramble to see the charming den of 16th-century conspirators.

DISTANCE 5.25miles (8.4km)	MINIMUM TIME 2hrs 30min
ASCENT/GRADIENT 70ft (21m) ▲▲▲	LEVEL OF DIFFICULTY +++

PATHS *Meadows and field paths, tracks and lanes, 11 stiles*

LANDSCAPE *Gentle farmland, picturesque, historic house*

SUGGESTED MAP *OS Explorer 204 Worcester & Droitwich Spa*

START/FINISH *Grid reference: SO 943543*

DOG FRIENDLINESS *Mixed farmland throughout*

PARKING *Roadside parking, Upton Snodsbury*

PUBLIC TOILETS *None en route*

WALK 10 DIRECTIONS

Begin on the primary school road, south of St Kenelm's Church (1874). Go west, past the school then some bungalows. Go diagonally right, then more right, down to conifers fringing the car park of the Oak on the A422. Cross over. Turn left, then right after 50yds (46m). In 100yds (91m) go ahead. Walk through a long field, scarcely gaining any height. Eventually leave by a pair of narrow metal gates, not a wide wooden one higher up.

> ### WHERE TO EAT AND DRINK
> There's a stores and post office in Upton Snodsbury. Near the start is the Oak, which has a beer garden. West a little, at the Peopleton turn, is Bant's, a pub restaurant.

Guy Fawkes was caught red-handed in the cellars of Parliament just after midnight on the night of 4–5 November in 1605. Historians cannot agree precisely why he was doing it. Was it a (misguided) attempt to spark the reinstatement of Catholicism, or a means of tarnishing the Jesuit movement by blaming them, thus strengthening the Protestant position? Guy Fawkes was born a Protestant, but converted to Catholicism in his early 20s. Aged 23, he went to the Netherlands to become a mercenary in the Spanish army-in-residence. He apparently believed that, given the right catalyst for change, Catholics in England would overthrow the King.

Now go straight ahead, joining a driveway. When 90yds (82m) beyond Bow Brook's bridge go half right, reaching a metal kissing gate beside the drive to Manor House. Despite a waymarker pointing to a stile close to Manor House, aim one pylon right of a rusty windmill to another metal kissing gate. Turn half left to a gate in trees. Turn right on this minor road for 650yds (594m). Now follow a right-hand field-edge (fingerpost). Just before the corner go through a gate to put it on your other side. At the next corner go through a gate

HUDDINGTON COURT

and turn right. At an opening into a big field aim 10yds (9m) left of a two-poled power pylon ahead. In and out of woodland, take the right-hand field-edge. At the bend ignore a double stile and three-planked bridge, going 20yds (18m) further to another stile. Go diagonally, to a waymarked stile 40yds (37m) before a metal gate. Emerge beside a black-and-white house and a greenhouse, beside Huddington Court.

Thomas Wintour (or Winter) and his brother, Robert, both lived at Huddington Court. They were two of at least 13 men involved in the conspiracy. Guy Fawkes was not the principal conspirator – just inept enough to get himself caught. It is claimed that he was found by people making a search, having received a tip-off in the form of an anonymous letter to a prominent Catholic, Lord Monteagle.

Turn left, not towards Huddington Court, crossing a dam at steps, to a minor road. Turn right. In 120yds (110m), turn into the Court's driveway. When it swings right, stop to admire the house. Huddington Court was built in the early 1500s, but greatly altered in 1584. The surrounding moat was probably dug for an earlier property on the site. The house belonged to the Wintours until 1658. Significantly, inside is a most secure priests' hole. Huddington Court is now privately owned.

In his reign Henry VIII's draconian Dissolution of the Monasteries had stripped them of their vast wealth, and he had established the Church of England, having broken away from the Pope. Later, Queen Elizabeth I introduced outrageous (but lucrative) fines for persons not attending Anglican services, so-called 'recusants'. A form of

WHILE YOU'RE THERE

Adjacent to the lawn of Huddington Court is the largely Norman and 14th-century Church of St James. Between his arrest and execution, Robert Wintour admitted that he had told the chaplain, a Jesuit priest, about the Gunpowder Plot.

'closet Catholicism' continued – almost literally, since harbouring a Catholic priest was punishable by death, and so some of them hid in priests' holes. Europe had also been incensed by Queen Elizabeth's execution of the fleeing Scottish Queen, Mary, a Catholic, in 1587. At the time of the Gunpowder Plot, James I, the Scottish King, had just inherited the English throne after the death of Elizabeth in 1603. Those who had not been killed after the discovery of Guy Fawkes were executed for treason in January 1606. These included Robert and Thomas Wintour and Guy Fawkes. They were hung, drawn and quartered (having probably been tortured first), then sundry body parts were exhibited.

Back at the minor road, walk on to Mill Farm. Follow the fingerpost. In a big field, aim for a prominent ash at a far woodland corner. Walk with the plantation on your left. At its second corner, turn left. At the end of this field keep within it, turning right. In 120yds (110m), go for 500yds (457m) diagonally towards trees, passing 50yds (46m) left of the first pylon. Through an aperture in the trees, reach a stile within 50yds (46m). Go half left, but on reaching a field boundary turn half right, staying within the field to walk parallel with Bow Wood. From the brow, continue with this field-edge on your left for 400yds (366m) to gates. A stone track leads to the A422 and thus Upton Snodsbury village.

Droitwich Spa: Turning Salt into Silver

*A walk through an historical town where salt
once made a fortune for a local family.*

DISTANCE 5.75miles (9.2km)   MINIMUM TIME 2hrs 30min

ASCENT/GRADIENT 230ft (70m) ▲▲▲   LEVEL OF DIFFICULTY ✦✦✦

PATHS *Pavements, field paths, stony tracks, 5 stiles*

LANDSCAPE *Agricultural lowlands, coppices, historical town*

SUGGESTED MAP *OS Explorer 204 Worcester & Droitwich Spa*

START/FINISH *Grid reference: SO 898631*

DOG FRIENDLINESS *Some country stretches but too urban to be much fun*

PARKING *Long-stay pay-and-display between Heritage Way and Saltway
(follow brown signs for Brine Baths)*

PUBLIC TOILETS *St Andrews Square Shopping centre*

Given that seawater is salty, it is not surprising to find salt pans by the Atlantic or on the Mediterranean coast. But how has salt been produced in Droitwich since prehistoric times? The answer is simply that the ground is rich in rock salt. The brine from the town's salt springs is far denser than sea water – 2.5lbs of salt could be extracted by boiling a gallon of Droitwich's brine (about 250g from each litre).

Salinae

Droitwich was an important Roman crossroads – the suggested map shows that the A38(T), the B4090 and the minor road to the north, Crutch Lane, all have Roman origins. They had a fort at Dodderhill (just north of Vines Park) and, when the railway was constructed in 1847, two mosaic pavements were stumbled upon. Later archaeological work found a Roman corridor house about 130ft (40m) long.

Salt tax was a good earner for the monarch, up until its abolition in 1825. Ownership of 25 salt-evaporating pans contributed to the wealth of the Wintour family, who gained notoriety in 1605 (see Walk 10).

The Salt King

In 1845, when aged 28, John Corbett used capital from his father's canal business's profits to buy and update a derelict salt works about 4.5 miles (7.2km) north-east, at Stoke Prior (see Walks 3 and 4). He did the right thing at the right time. His works, Europe's largest, made him a fortune, much of which he pumped back into the company, improving working conditions and raising wages (to the extent that wives no longer needed to work), and also into the area, Droitwich Spa in particular. In France, in 1855, he met Anna (or Hannah) O'Meara, who lived in Paris with her French mother and Irish father. Corbett married her the following year. They had six children. Such was her apparent craving for France that he commissioned an architect to build him a French château, Château Impney, completed in 1875 for a staggering £247,000. Despite this, they separated after 28 years of marriage. In 1879 Corbett bought, and vastly improved, St Andrew's House. He renamed it the Raven Hotel, after the raven on the Corbett family's coat of arms (from the French for raven, '*le corbeau*'… which sounds a bit like 'Corbett').

To some extent, the use of ice (see Walk 6) and, later, refrigeration, as a means of preserving meats and other foods contributed to the decline of Droitwich's salt production, which ceased in 1922. Most recently, in a triumph of shopping over heritage, the Salters' Shopping Centre has been 'rebranded' as St Andrews Square.

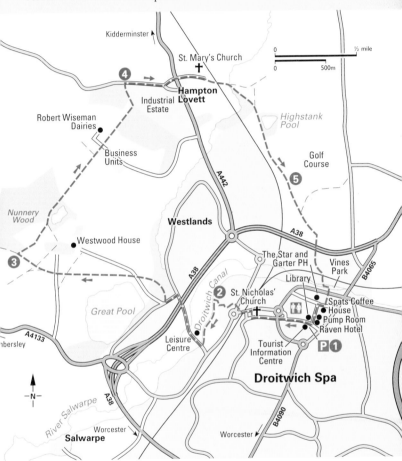

WALK 11 DIRECTIONS

❶ Begin outside the library with your back to the Raven Hotel. Go west, along Victoria Square. Cross Heritage Way into Ombersley Street East. When it bends go straight on, passing a medical centre. After an underpass proceed to St Nicholas' Church. Go beyond the churchyard then right, to take another underpass. Turn left. Take the road over the railway to a mini-roundabout, filtering right to go through a third underpass. Walk for 50yds (46m) to a fence corner, near a lamppost. Turn left. In 30yds (27m) turn right. At the bottom of this cul-de-sac, Westmead Close, turn left. Soon take Ledwych Close, on the right. At the canal you are effectively out of Droitwich Spa.

2 Turn left. At the bridge turn right, passing sports facilities and schools. Turn left just beyond the A38 bridge, into Westwood Way. In 110yds (100m) reach the Westwood House slip road. Facing some allotments, take a gate to the left. Beyond this woodland reach a driveway. Cross a truly enormous arable field. Over a track and another driveway, finally reach a corner of Nunnery Wood.

3 Turn sharply right. Electric fencing shepherds you between paddocks before you veer left to walk briefly through Nunnery Wood. (Ignore tracks left.) Aim for two gates beside trees on the skyline. Keep straight on for 0.5 mile (800m), near Robert Wiseman Dairies on the left, then curving left past an industrial estate to reach Doverdale Lane.

4 Turn right. Just before a '30' speed-limit sign, fork left. Cross the A442. Walk through the hamlet of Hampton Lovett to St Mary's Church. (It is asymmetrical, having a curved Norman column on its left side.) Take the meadow path under the railway. In 140yds (128m), at a footbridge, bear right, along a field-edge. Keep following this general, waymarked line for over 0.5 mile (800m), walking outside the right edge of the trees beside Highstank Pool. Go forward with hedgerow

on your left; when it stops abruptly aim across a large field to clip corner greenery – young evergreens shielding a golf tee.

5 Keeping the same line, cross a vast field – in fact, just more of the same field! – to a small new metal gate. Now aim slightly left to another metal gate. Follow the road under the A38 into a housing estate. Go forward, then down for about 150yds (137m), to find a tarmac path running between Nos 49 and 53 (51 is hidden). Go through two kissing gates flanking the level crossing. Turn left to The Gardeners Arms. Here turn right over the River Salwarpe, into Vines Park. Veer left to cross the Droitwich Canal. Cross this busy road and walk down the right side of a supermarket to High Street – in front of you is Spats Coffee House. Turn right, passing Tower Hill, then left into St Andrew's Street and then back to the start of the walk.

Sights and Smells of Worcester City

The city of Worcester is known for Sir Edward Elgar, its battle, its sauce, its porcelain and its racecourse; but what of its largely unsung hero?

DISTANCE 2.5 miles (4km)   MINIMUM TIME 1hr 30min

ASCENT/GRADIENT Negligible ▲▲▲   LEVEL OF DIFFICULTY +++

PATHS City streets and tarmac riverside path

LANDSCAPE Urban with riverside

SUGGESTED MAP OS Explorer 204 Worcester & Droitwich Spa

START/FINISH Grid reference: SO 846548

DOG FRIENDLINESS Not dog friendly (except short stretch by river)

PARKING Long-stay pay-and-display car parks at New Road, Tybridge Street and Croft Road (and elsewhere)

PUBLIC TOILETS Near start at Croft Road and bus station; several elsewhere

The development of Lea & Perrins' Worcester Sauce was largely accidental. The story goes that the two chemists, who ran a store between Broad Street and Bank Street (just off High Street), were asked to make up a recipe brought back from abroad in the 1820s. This they did, making an extra jar for themselves. Finding it excessively hot, they put the jar aside. Some years later they stumbled upon it and, quite bravely, sipped it – eureka! It had mellowed to a pleasant piquancy. The secrecy surrounding the recipe is (apparently) retained, eccentrically but effectively, firstly by employing any given worker only on part of the process, and secondly by giving the ingredients meaningless code names. HP Foods, which is now owned by Heinz, bought the business back in 1930. It has since gone on to achieve worldwide brand status.

New Street

Keep your eyes directed at least 10ft (3m) off the ground and New Street – actually rather old – is a visual feast. In the late 18th century, many merchants migrated from here, making their houses tenements and workshops. The merchants left partly because of the stench. Nowadays the most likely smell wafting down New Street is of fast food. An 1832 report said of The Shambles that 'filth of all description remains until it is perfectly alive', and in 1846 another said that in parts of Worcester 'pools of liquid filth perpetually stagnate the surface.'

Sir Charles Hastings

Charles Hastings was a brilliant youth. He attended anatomy school in London when 16, became house surgeon to Worcester Infirmary aged 18, went to Edinburgh University aged 21, and returned to Worcester Infirmary. (He declined a professorship at Edinburgh.) Ahead of his time, Hastings believed that the state should be responsible for the health of its public. He conducted much research into what nowadays would be called 'occupational health' – of local porcelain workers, glovers, and salt workers, for example – and founded the Provincial Medical and Surgical Association. Twenty-four years later, with Hastings still at the helm, legislation formally established this body as the British Medical Association, which still oversees the work of medical practitioners today. It is said that he attended every case during the three cholera outbreaks in 1832, 1849 and 1853.

A True Philanthropist

In 1854 Dr Hastings put much of his own money into innovative 'modern dwellings' (long-demolished, off Copenhagen Street) for artisans. He at least had the satisfaction of seeing the local death rate fall by 45 per cent in a decade. However, he still had a fight on his hands to persuade the city council to provide clean water. Amazingly, legislation compelling local councils to do this did not reach the statute books until 1872.

He benefited the people of Worcester in several other ways too, such as by founding a natural history museum in the city. His grave lies in Worcester's Astwood Cemetery. When he died in 1866, aged 72, Sir Charles Hastings was Worcester's most lauded citizen; at that time Edward Elgar was only nine years old. One could argue as to which brought about the greater benefit to Worcester city.

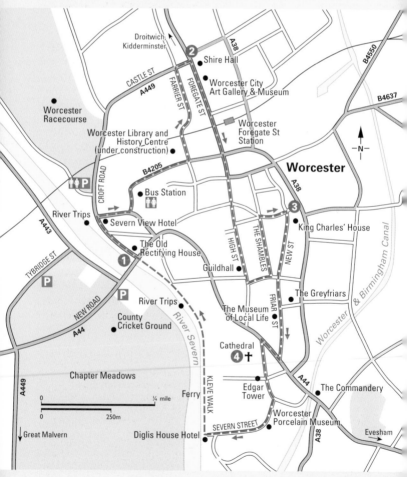

WALK 12 DIRECTIONS

1 The described route begins at the city side of the road bridge, but you can pick it up anywhere – at The Commandery or the Guildhall, for example – depending on where you have parked. Turn left, passing The Old Rectifying House (wine bar). Turn right after the Severn View Hotel, then left, in front of the bus station, following the road round to pass The Butts Dig (archaeological site). Turn left along Farrier Street, right into Castle Street, reaching the northern extremity of the route at its junction with Foregate Street.

2 Go right along Foregate Street, passing the Shire Hall and the Worcester City Art Gallery & Museum. Continue along The Cross and into the pedestrianised area called High Street. Turn left into Pump Street. (Elgar's statue stands close to his father's piano shop, at the southern end of High Street.) Turn left again, into The Shambles. At a junction turn right into Mealcheapen Street. Another right turn and you're in New Street (which later becomes Friar Street).

3 Head down this partial time warp as slowly as you can, admiring The Greyfriars (a National Trust property) in particular, for a dual carriageway awaits you at the end. Turn right, then cross over carefully, to visit the cathedral.

4 Leave the cathedral along College Precincts to the fortified gateway known as Edgar Tower. (It is named after the 10th-century King Edgar, but was actually built in the 14th century. Go through this gateway to see College Green.) Continue, along what is now Severn Street which, unsurprisingly, leads to the River Severn. Turn right, to complete your circuit, by following Kleve Walk, a leafy waterside avenue; this section floods frequently, as does the county cricket ground opposite at great cost to the club's revenue.

Kingsford Forest Park and Villages

*A Worcestershire backwater that
once knew busier times.*

DISTANCE 5.5 miles (8.8km)   **MINIMUM TIME** 2hrs 30min

ASCENT/GRADIENT 410ft (125m) ▲▲▲   **LEVEL OF DIFFICULTY** +++

PATHS Forest rides, meadows, minor roads, village streets,
canal tow path, 9 stiles

LANDSCAPE Mostly pastures and woodland in rolling countryside

SUGGESTED MAP OS Explorer 218 Wyre Forest & Kidderminster
or 219 Wolverhampton & Dudley

START/FINISH Grid reference: SO 835820

DOG FRIENDLINESS Much fun in woods but horses and sheep elsewhere

PARKING Blakeshall Lane car park, Kingsford Forest Park

PUBLIC TOILETS None en route

On this and other walks you may come across dense spindley woodland that somehow 'doesn't look right'. Such areas of trees may be to the oak what a pile of stones is to an old church: a ruin. The occurrence of the word 'coppice' on a map – Solcum Coppice, Gloucester Coppice – often indicates a woodland of historical importance to the local economy. With its proximity to the industries of the West Midlands, local charcoal production (especially in the Wyre Forest) was considerable.

Invention or Discovery?

Is charcoal an invention or a discovery? Probably it was 'discovered' by accident, and its subsequent uses were invented. It is wood that has been incompletely burned (in a controlled way) by being deprived of much of the oxygen that would otherwise render it a pile of ashes. Woods used for charcoal-making include hazel – a favourite because of its prolific re-growth – ash, oak and alder buckthorn, among others.

A Slow Process

The raw material was cut and left to dry or 'season' for several months before use. This, together with how well and for how long the 'kiln' was burning, were key factors in determining the yield – 15–25 per cent was good, and 30 per cent exceptional. The kiln was a temporary structure, essentially a mound or dome of logs carefully constructed around a central airway, the whole being covered with turf, ideal since the roots of the grass bound the soil together tightly, and the turfs were easier to handle than soil on its own. Turf would also be used to cover the airway once a fire had been established at the core. It could take several days to complete the charcoal-making process. Of course, much of the weight lost is evaporated moisture. When re-ignited, the charcoal burns with an intensity capable of smelting metal, forging iron, and making glass, as well as blackening your burger. Gunpowder is concocted from three ingredients – charcoal, sulphur and saltpetre (potassium nitrate). Only when the coal derivative, coke, was introduced was charcoal superseded as an intensive heat source. (Coke later gave way to oil and gas, which also have the advantage of being easier to control.)

Charcoal in the 21st Century

Don't think that your summertime barbeques are necessarily being fuelled by British-grown trees, for in all probability they aren't. Over 90 per cent of the charcoal sold in Britain is imported, a statistic that upsets environmentalists greatly, since much of it is sourced from the notoriously unsustained tropical rain forests. In Britain, depending on the species, trees should be coppiced every 7–20 years. The British countryside has a vast stock of growing wood that could be managed in a sustainable way, that is, harvested cyclically, without reducing the total tree stock, but the high income expectation of labour makes it an uneconomic proposition. Or does it? At the last count the BioRegional Charcoal Company, a marketing co-operative, had over 25 producers.

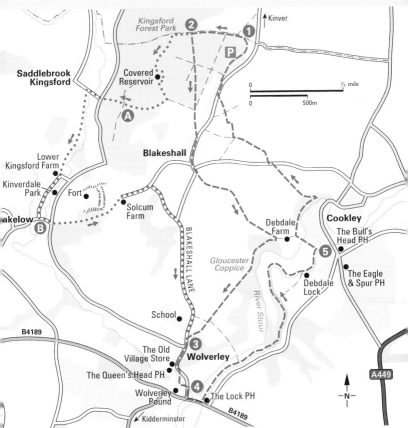

WALK 13 DIRECTIONS

1 Take the track inside the northern edge of the forest park

for 550yds (503m), to a point about 80yds (73m) beyond the end of Kinver Edge Farm's extensive garden. To the left is a wide glade,

WALK 13

falling gently; ahead rises the woodland track (Walk 14).

2 Turn left, down the ride. In 275yds (251m), at a five-way junction, go ahead (not along a slight right fork). Join a farm track. At a road turn right, through Blakeshall. After 300yds (274m), at a right-hand bend near power lines, take a stile into a field. Keep a hedge on your right, following yellow waymarkers into a small valley. When about 300yds (274m) from Debdale Farm, move up to the fence, following it to a corner. Enter Gloucester Coppice at a gate and stile. Follow this track, soon more defined, all the way to the southern end of Blakeshall Lane (where Walk 14 rejoins).

3 Turn left, descending into Wolverley. See the footbridge alongside The Queen's Head and The Old Village Store, but take the other one. Reach the Church of St John the Baptist by iron gates, zig-zagging up the concreted footpath through a deep cutting (if the gates are locked use the road). Leave the churchyard by modern steps. Go down the meadow opposite (with a fingerpost) to a minor road.

4 Turn right. At the B4189, turn left. In front of The Lock public house turn left, along the tow path. After about 1.25miles (2km) is Debdale Lock, partly hewn into the rock. Some 220yds (201m) further, just before the steel wheel factory, is a stile.

5 Turn left here along a track. (Alternatively continue for 150yds (137m) for refreshments in Cookley.) At a T-junction after a coniferous avenue, turn right on a broad gravel track. After about 350yds (320m) turn left (waymarker), up some wooden steps, into trees. Go up the left-hand edge of one field and the centre of another to a road. Turn left for just 15yds (14m), then right. Some 400yds (366m) along this hedged lane turn right, contrary to the blue arrow pointing ahead. At the next stile wiggle left, then right. Proceed straight ahead at a junction to the road. Turn right. In 150yds (137m), move left into the trees to re-enter the country park. Two paths run parallel to the road – both lead back to the car park.

WHAT TO LOOK OUT FOR

Compared with Wolverley's other buildings, St John the Baptist Church is surprisingly ugly – in a pretty churchyard, this drab lump has brick arches in its windows reminiscent of a railway viaduct. More memorable, although grim, is a monument to five siblings, all of whom died between the ages of nine months and six years in the late 18th century. On a brighter note, if the church is unlocked, you'll find inside some stained-glass windows made by William Morris's company (See Walk 1) and an effigy of a knight, well-preserved given its 14th-century vintage. Just down to the left of the (busy) mini-roundabout is Wolverley Pound. In part cut into the sandstone, it was used as a corral for stray animals until 'ransomed' by their owners.

A Longer Walk in Kingsford Forest Park

This extension, looping through a forest park, includes two short sections of the Worcestershire Way.
See map and information panel for Walk 13

DISTANCE 7.25miles (11.7km) **MINIMUM TIME** 3hrs
ASCENT/GRADIENT 560ft (171m) ▲▲▲ **LEVEL OF DIFFICULTY** +++

WALK 14 DIRECTIONS (Walk 13 option)

At Point **2** continue for 160yds (146m) to a fingerpost that includes 'Staffordshire Way', indicating the county border. Turn left down this good track. Soon fork left of a fenced-off, covered reservoir. At a junction turn right, but in 40yds (37m) – see Severn Trent Water's 'Blakeshall' sign through the fence – turn left. After 160yds (146m) at the forest edge, turn right on the inner path, that is, through a single-bar gate, passing a bench 30yds (27m) beyond it. Go along here for 425yds (389m) to reach a T-junction, Point **A**.

Here, do not turn left along the Worcestershire Way, but turn right for just 20yds (18m), then left on a path running through pines and silver birch. Reach a road junction within 200yds (183m) and go down the stem of the T-junction. Within 160yds (146m) take the waymarked path left, opposite the house, 'Saddlebrook Kingsford'. This green band improves to become a metalled road. Turn right, passing Lower Kingsford Farm, to reach a T-junction, Point **B**.

Here turn left, crossing over to the pavement set back from the road. At the next T-junction cross the road and go straight on, along a works access road, to reach a gate into woods. Ascend gently. Beside a house with decorative walling, join a lane that goes straight ahead. At the next junction turn right, away from the Worcestershire Way, following this minor road (becoming Blakeshall Lane) towards Wolverley. Shortly before you reach the village pass Wolverley High School, then rejoin Walk 13.

WHILE YOU'RE THERE

If you visit the Bodenham Arboretum (north-west of Drakelow), be sure to allow enough time to do justice to its 156 acres (63ha) and over 3,000 tree and shrub species. The arboretum is open from February half-term until Christmas, Wednesdays to Sundays 11am to 5pm, plus Mondays and Tuesdays in October (for autumn colours), and Thursday evenings from May to August. Dogs on lead are welcome in the grounds.

Upton on the flood plains of the Severn

An easy walk to a black-and-white village, returning by the river.

WALK 15

> DISTANCE 5.75miles (9.2km) MINIMUM TIME 2hrs 15min
>
> ASCENT/GRADIENT 80ft (24m) ▲▲▲ LEVEL OF DIFFICULTY ✦✦✦
>
> PATHS Meadows, lanes, tracks, village streets, riverside, 9 stiles
>
> LANDSCAPE Low-lying meadows, fruit farms, villages, small town
>
> SUGGESTED MAP OS Explorer 190 Malvern Hills & Bredon Hill
>
> START/FINISH Grid reference: SO 850402
>
> DOG FRIENDLINESS Some opportunities for trustworthy dogs to be off lead
>
> PARKING Free car park opposite Church of St Peter and St Paul
>
> PUBLIC TOILETS In town centre

WALK 15 DIRECTIONS

Begin away from Upton, along the A4104. The 'new' Church of St Peter and St Paul was built in 1878–9 in a neo-Gothic style. Within 100yds (91m) take the old road right, skirting sports fields. Just before this rejoins the A4104, turn right again. At the bend near modern office buildings take stiles on the right. Near the field end go left, ascending through a plantation. At a sunken lane turn left, to houses and a street.

Walk beside a playing field, then turn right, passing a children's play area. Take the second public footpath on the right, signposted 'Hanley Castle', later through an orchard. Cross a road, going down another orchard row, admiring the Discovery apples and Czar plums of Clive's Fruit Farm. At the end move left to cross the old railway track by wooden steps, noting the railway company's iron-and-concrete stiles. Follow a sunken lane. Turn left at a road. At a junction turn right, soon taking a gravel driveway left between two bridges. Go right of the house to a stile beyond its sheds. Pass some hazel coppice on the right. A huge conifer marks Hanley Castle's site.

The castle that stood here was, in the 13th century, part of the Earl of Gloucester's estate. It was mostly demolished, when already a ruin, at the time of Henry VIII, but some residual stone was later used to repair Upton's bridge.

Near the conifer turn right to cross a stream. Go through a gate and stile beyond it. In a few paces turn left through a rusty kissing gate. Take the left-hand field-edge and then enter the churchyard, ignoring waymarkers.

WHERE TO EAT AND DRINK

The Three Kings Inn in Hanley Castle serves snacks and traditional ales. In Upton there are many choices. The route passes three riverside pubs – The Plough Inn, The King's Head and The Swan Hotel. The Olde Bell House Tea Rooms are in New Street.

UPTON UPON SEVERN

The chunk of brickwork – the central tower, the north chapel, and the chancel – was added in 1674, whereas the stonework is largely 14th century. Near by, the timber frames of the almshouses are from 1600, but they were rebuilt in the early 19th century. The school has been added to, piecemeal, with varying degrees of architectural sense, since its foundation in 1544.

Walk down the village street to the B4211. Turn right along the pavement for 220yds (201m). Cross at the cross. Quay Lane leads to the river. Turn right, soon edging a vast arable field.

Upton's craftsmen are believed to have aided the Parliamentarians in their preparations for the Battle of Worcester in 1651 (see Walk 20). They built two pontoons, which were hauled by the Parliamentary army from Upton to the Teme–Severn confluence. They used these two 'bridges of boats' to cross each river, giving them a great strategic advantage. The tower of Upton's old church, built on a 13th-century base, was the scene of a skirmish a few days before the decisive battle. The remainder was demolished in 1937; a 14th-century effigy and several memorials were transferred to the new church.

After a long 0.5 mile (800m), rejoin the B4211's pavement. Go under Upton Bridge, past its predecessor's site and three pubs.

Here the River Severn is only 36ft (11m) above sea level. During 22 July 2007 a gauge at Saxon's Lode, just 1.5 miles (2.4km) downriver, measured a whopping 19.5ft (5.94m). This is reckoned to have been a 1-in-150-years event (and exceeded the 18.9ft (5.76m) of March 1947, caused by melting snow). Upton gained notoriety – dubbed 'Upton under Severn' – when its flood defences, stored somewhere up the M5, could not be delivered in time… due to surface flooding. According to the Environment Agency, had these barriers been deployed they would, anyway, have been overtopped! Up in the Welsh mountains, near where the River Severn rises, is Llyn Clywedog Reservoir. It was built in the 1960s to control the Severn's flow, but, even boasting the highest mass concrete dam in Britain, it can only hold so much.

WHILE YOU'RE THERE

Severn Leisure Cruises have a huge boat at Upton. The Tudor House Museum at 16 Church Street focuses on local history. At the end of June, Upton hosts a three-day Jazz Festival, attracting performers from diverse locations such as the USA, Hungary and Norway.

Keep beside the river on a road. A gate leads on to Upper Ham. After 750yds (686m), at a fishery sign, turn right. A kissing gate gives on to a vehicular track. At the first tarmac road go straight ahead.

At the crossroads, turn right into School Lane, all the way to the town centre. (Turn right for the tourist information centre in High Street.) If you learn nothing else from this walk, please remember that the 1850 Roman Catholic Chapel of St Joseph in School Lane was built by a C Hansom, the brother of taxi cab designer Joseph Hansom, and that the racing driver Nigel Mansell was born in Upton upon Severn on 8 August 1953. Turn left along Old Street to return to your car.

WALK 16

Ombersley and Holt Fleet

Explore an estate park and the banks of the River Severn.

DISTANCE 5.75miles (9.2km) MINIMUM TIME 2hrs 30min

ASCENT/GRADIENT 200ft (61m) ▲▲▲ LEVEL OF DIFFICULTY +++

PATHS *Riverside paths, field paths and tracks, village street, 6 stiles*

LANDSCAPE *Estate parkland, riverside meadows and general farmland*

SUGGESTED MAP *OS Explorer 204 Worcester & Droitwich Spa*

START/FINISH *Grid reference: SO 845630*

DOG FRIENDLINESS *Few off-lead opportunities unless very obedient*

PARKING *Towards southern end of road through Ombersley on eastern side (no southbound exit from village)*

PUBLIC TOILETS *None en route*

Ombersley must have been awful before the bypass, but now it verges on the tranquil. Ombersley Court was built in the 1720s. Apparently it has a superb interior, but the nearest you'll get to even a reasonable view of it is at the far end of the churchyard (beside a grim memorial tree). Sited on the Ombersley Park Estate, St Andrew's Church was built 100 years after Ombersley Court, but in the decorated style of the early 14th century, presumably to reflect the fragment of the original church (now a mausoleum) behind it.

Silence of the Owls

Along the river towards Holt Bridge, to your right (and left also) is a classic stretch of woodland, adorning the steep slopes of the great River Severn's flood plain. If you were to walk along here at dusk you could hope to see an owl, possibly even a barn owl, but you probably wouldn't. A survey conducted in Worcestershire in 1932 found 184 breeding pairs of barn owls, but a similar survey in 1985 found just 32. There were numerous reasons for its decline. Part of the blame is apportioned to the grubbing out of the hedgerows, thereby removing a good habitat for small mammals. However, much is apportioned to intensive agriculture's use of pesticides, moving along the food chain so that, by the time a barn owl has eaten 100 or so slightly contaminated but well mammals (mice, shrews, voles), the cumulative dosage of pesticide is fatal.

The goal of the Worcestershire Barn Owl Society (WBOS) is to reverse the trend, partly by breeding barn owls and releasing them in carefully chosen locations. Barn owls are quite happy in tree hollows but, no, they rarely approve of barn conversions. The WBOS builds and erects nest boxes in strategic places to compensate for the loss – you can even buy or sponsor one. Like other owls, the barn owl flies silently, a useful hunting trick, achieved by having soft tips to its wing feathers – these tips effectively deaden any airflow noise.

Holt Fleet

The bridge at Holt Fleet replaced a ferry. It was the last in Worcestershire to cease taking tolls. (In Herefordshire tolls are still taken at the 1802 Whitney Bridge, near Walk 47.) Such was the belief in a German invasion that mines were laid under the Holt Fleet Bridge during the Second World War. The Holt Fleet pub was built well before the bridge, and benefited greatly from the day-tripper business, being the northern terminus for paddle steamer trips from Worcester, about 7 miles (11.3km) to the south. These trips ran until the 1930s. In contrast, The Wharf Inn, on the east bank, marks the site of a coal wharf. Holt Lock, a little way upstream, was completed in 1844.

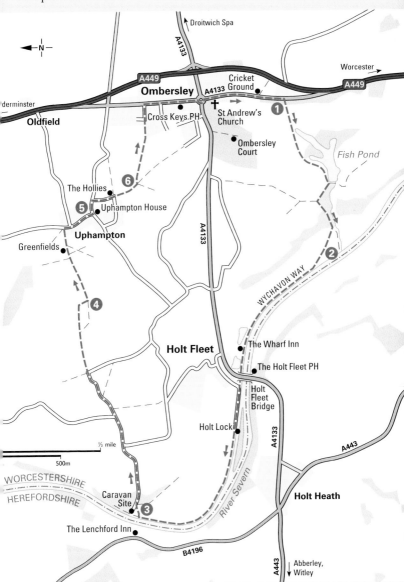

WALK 16 DIRECTIONS

WALK 16

❶ To the south of the village, and beyond the cricket ground, take a path on the right, signposted 'Turn Mill'. This is the Wychavon Way. Briefly in trees, walk across a meadow to a stile beside a willow. Go along the left-hand field-edges, and briefly by the water's edge. At the corner of the fish pond go a few paces beyond a waymarker to a track. Turn left, following this track right in 80yds (73m). It becomes a sunken path through delicious woodland. Cross a meadow to the river.

> ### WHAT TO LOOK OUT FOR
> The very ordinary and workmanlike single arch bridge at Holt was built by Thomas Telford in 1828 – he was responsible for six others over the Severn. It is the only Severn crossing between Stourport and Worcester. A caravan site on the other side of the river has static caravans set on pillars, as a flood limitation measure.

❷ Turn right. In 0.75 mile (1.2km) you'll pass two fishing pools to reach Holt Fleet Bridge. Go under this, continuing for 1 mile (1.6km), passing the staffed Holt Lock. When opposite The Lenchford Inn you'll come to a riverside stile.

❸ Don't go over this stile; instead, turn right. In the field corner join the access road. At a junction go straight ahead on the public road. In 650yds (594m), at a right-hand bend, keep this line by moving left, on to a farm track. It's over 0.25 mile (400m) to the top of this field. Keep on the track, seeing a rusty shed ahead. When you are 30yds (27m) before it, turn right. Now, in 90yds (82m) go left, through a gate.

> ### WHERE TO EAT AND DRINK
> On the route, The Wharf Inn has a riverside terrace and beer garden, and some children's play equipment. Close by, across the bridge, is The Holt Fleet. In Ombersley, at its northern end, is Cross Keys. Further down in a cluster are the quirkily named The Venture In (restaurant), The Kings Arms and the refurbished Crown & Sandys.

❹ What could be mistaken for a golf course fairway turns out to be an enormous garden. Aim to pass to the right of the house called Greenfields, and a children's wooden watchtower, walking beside a walled vegetable garden. Keep ahead to go down its private, brick-paved driveway. Turn right, passing several black-and-white houses, to a T-junction – Uphampton House is in front of you.

❺ Turn left for 110yds (100m), then turn right, uphill. In 150yds (137m), at The Hollies, don't bend right but go straight ahead, on a shingly track. About 220yds (201m) further, the main track bends right, a rough track goes ahead and a public footpath goes half left.

❻ Take the public footpath option, along a field-edge. Continue through a small area of market garden, reaching a cul-de-sac. Shortly turn right, along the village street. There are many houses to look at, the churches of St Andrew (current and former), and several points of refreshment to delay your return to your car.

Hartlebury Common and Stourport-on-Severn

*Cut through a Georgian 'new town'
before striding out across a common.*

DISTANCE 3.25 miles (5.3km) MINIMUM TIME 1hr 30min

ASCENT/GRADIENT 328ft (100m) ▲▲▲ LEVEL OF DIFFICULTY ✦✦✦

PATHS Tow path, tracks, good paths, some streets

LANDSCAPE Urban, watery, and common with extensive views

SUGGESTED MAP OS Explorer 218 Wyre Forest & Kidderminster
or 219 Wolverhampton & Dudley

START/FINISH Grid reference: SO 820704

DOG FRIENDLINESS Good on common and tow path, not much fun in town

PARKING Hartlebury Common South Car Park on A4025 (poorly signed;
a white height restriction bar spans narrow entrance)

PUBLIC TOILETS None en route

You will understand the rise and fall of Stourport-on-Severn if you look at a map of England. The infrastructural advantage realised by the opening of the Staffordshire and Worcestershire Canal was to link the River Severn with the rivers Trent and Mersey.

Horse Power, Canal Power

Canals were conceived when road transport was not only uncomfortable for passengers but also extremely slow for goods, and railways had yet to be invented. Roads were in a poor condition, invariably worsened by the winter months. River transport was, at least, an option along the Severn. (In comparison, Herefordshire's River Wye was usually too low in the summer months to give sufficient draught to even a small sailing barge.) A horse and cart could carry perhaps 300lb (136kg). Along a canal tow path, a horse could haul a barge carrying a vastly greater burden – up to 50 tons (50,679kg), a more than 300-fold weight advantage. Although the horse moved slowly, it is easy to see how those with money to invest fashionably threw it at all manner of canal projects (see Walks 26 and 27). For Joe Public the main outcome was cheaper coal.

Steam Horse

In 1771, when the Staffordshire and Worcestershire Canal opened, Stourport grew up, becoming what we might now call a 'new town'. Apart from the barge and boat building, foundries and carpet factories, for example, were also opened. After just four decades, trade was hit by the new Worcester and Birmingham Canal, which had itself been 24 years in the making (see Walk 3). Railway proliferation sent Stourport into further decline.

When the canals were nationalised in 1948, the days of commercial canal activity were already numbered. In the case of the Worcester and Birmingham Canal, the last two companies to use the canal regularly stopped in the early 1960s; they were Worcester's Royal Porcelain (for

WALK

17

coal) and Cadbury's of Bournville (for chocolate crumb). The commercial activity seen on the canal nowadays is of a totally different sort – canal-boat cruising is an enormously popular holiday choice.

Birth of the Family Narrow Boat

In a sense we have the railways to thank for canal-boat holidays. Trains were to prove the undoing of the canals (as lorries were to prove the undoing of the railways), but the initial response by the canal operators was to cut prices, and this meant cutting costs. Labour was not in short supply, so wages for boatmen were cut; their response, since so much of their time was spent on the water anyway, was to shed the burden of rent-paying by bringing their families on board their barges.

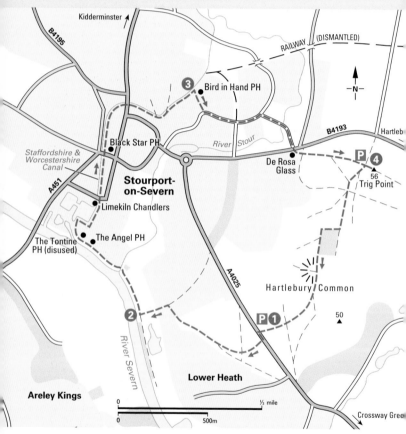

WALK 17 DIRECTIONS

① Cross the A4025. Turn left for just 25yds (23m) to take a footpath. Strike across this bottom part of Hartlebury Common: you'll see some buildings in the far distance. Veer right, roughly following power lines, through

silver birches, to find a sandy track at the back of some houses. At a modern housing estate join the tarmac briefly, aiming for a dirt track beyond the 'Britannia Gardens' sign and after Globe House. Turn left down a tarmac footpath, initially with wooden paling on the left, to the river.

STOURPORT-ON-SEVERN

2 Turn right. In 650yds (594m) you'll reach a lock and Stourport's canal basins. You'll probably want to spend some time exploring here but the route is neither across the two-plank walkway at the upper lock gate, nor the upper brick bridge with timber and metal railings; instead take the neat brick-paved path to circumnavigate The Tontine (see What to Look Out For). Now skirt the Upper Basin, passing Limekiln Chandlers. Across York Street join the tow path. Follow this for a little under 0.75 mile (1.2km), leaving it at the Bird in Hand, before a defunct brick railway bridge.

3 Go down Holly Road, then half left into Mill Road, following it for 0.25 mile (400m), over a mini-roundabout and across the River Stour to the B4193. Cross and go to the left of De Rosa Glass to take a narrow, sandy, uphill path back on to the common. Soon, at a fork, go left, keeping in this direction as the ground levels and a parking area lies to the left. Go ahead to find, adjacent to a wire fence, the unpainted trig point.

4 Now retrace your steps for about 90yds (82m), passing a wooden waymarker, to a junction. Here turn left, away from the car park. Again in about 90yds (82m), at a T-junction with a marker post, turn left (signposted 'Heather Trail'). At the corner of a conifer plantation, 275yds (251m) further, turn right. After 100yds (91m) turn left, then in 220yds (201m), just after the far end of the plantation, enjoy views to the west. Now 65yds (60m) beyond this viewpoint, take the right option at a subtle fork. Go forward on this for another 250yds (229m), until an opening. Here step very carefully over a pair of exposed and disused (but not actually hazardous) pipes. Follow the sandy track slanting downhill for 110yds (100m), then swing right, now making a beeline for the car park.

Great Witley Circuit: a Sneeze in the Trees

A mostly woodland walk up and down some of Worcestershire's lesser-known hills.

DISTANCE 4.75 miles (7.7km)   MINIMUM TIME 2hrs 30min

ASCENT/GRADIENT 1,150ft (350m) ▲▲▲   LEVEL OF DIFFICULTY +++

PATHS Woodland paths, field paths, tracks, 12 stiles

LANDSCAPE Wooded hills and farmed valleys

SUGGESTED MAP OS Explorer 204 Worcester & Droitwich Spa

START/FINISH Grid reference: SO 752662

DOG FRIENDLINESS Will be driven wild by geese! Running in woods but lead needed over grazing land

PARKING Large car park of The Hundred House Hotel (as a courtesy please phone beforehand, tel 01299 896888)

PUBLIC TOILETS None en route

What sort of walker are you – 'any weather' or 'fair weather'? Or are you a 'low pollen count walker', suffering from hay fever? Grasses are the most common cause, but just about any pollen can produce allergenic reactions. Between 10 per cent and 35 per cent of us suffer from 'pollinosis' (allergy to pollen), but these reactions may be species-specific. In addition, some species of tree seem to have more potent pollen than others, birch in particular. Pollen is typically released from grasses from May to August, oilseed rape from April to June, and stinging nettles from May to mid-September. These are all good reasons for getting out walking in the winter but, if you are afflicted in January, it could be pollen from alder or hazel, and in March it could be birch. Studies show that the season for birch pollen has shifted to five days earlier every decade over the past 30 years, a clear indication of global warming. Put that way it may not seem much, but it's actually half a month.

Bronchitis

The National Pollen Research Unit (NPRU), at University College, Worcester, is at the forefront of the science of 'aerobiology'. Supplying pollen forecasts is just one of the NPRU's diverse activities; others include studying changes in pollen seasons in relation to climate change, and studying asthma in relation to fungi and house-dust mites in homes. Of particular concern is chronic bronchitis – properly, chronic obstructive pulmonary disease (COPD). It is caused primarily by smoking, but there are other, secondary factors at work – this must be the case as in some southern European countries people smoke more but there is less COPD. One possible factor is Britain's higher humidity. One piece of research focused on whether or not (and if so, how) mists and fogs can increase the occurrence of COPD.

Happy Geese

From early spring until mid-December the lane around Walsgrove Farm is awash with geese – about 3,500 of them. (You will see turkeys too.) This is

GREAT WITLEY

just another of the diverse activities you can come across in the back lanes of Worcestershire and Herefordshire. They are prepared for sale using an on-site 'low throughput processing unit'. Until then, these free-range birds are allowed to range very freely. Nearly all are destined for the Christmas table, primarily through butchers and retailers, but you can buy one at the farm gate (September-Decemeber) too.

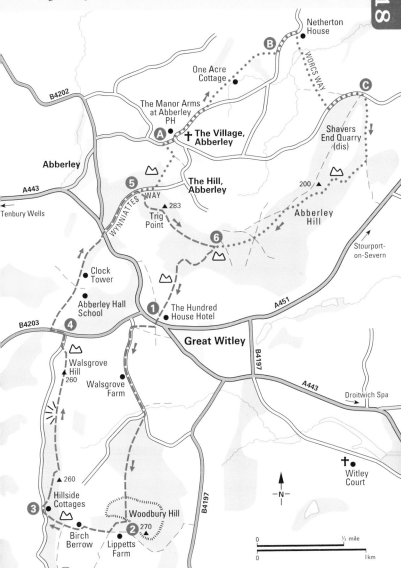

WALK 18 DIRECTIONS

❶ Cross the A451 with great care. Through an opening, strike sharply right, aiming for the

hedge end beside the last house. Turn left on this lane. Walk for 0.5 mile (800m) along here, soon passing firstly Walsgrove Farm and secondly (most of the year) thousands of strutting, wailing geese. Do not turn right up a lane but go half right, taking the path that becomes a beautiful wooded avenue, to the top of Woodbury Hill. Reach the second information board.

2 Go forward just a few paces to turn right at a marker post. In 50yds (46m), turn right. Continue forward to walk along the inside edge of a wood. Skirt to the left of the buildings at Birch Berrow, resuming on a gravel, fenced-in path. Take two stiles. Go steeply down, taking a stile into thick pines. In pasture again, descend further, reaching The Woodlands' driveway and a T-junction. Turn right along the tarmac road for 75yds (69m) to a marker post just past 1 Hillside Cottages.

WHILE YOU'RE THERE

Visit spectacular Witley Court, 1.25 miles (2km) south-east of Great Witley. The Court's 'in-your-face' architecture, mostly Victorian, is just stunning. Only the skeleton remains, since its flesh was burned by a fire in 1937. English Heritage describe it as their number one ruin.

---

3 Turn right again, back uphill. Continue north for nearly 1 mile (1.6km), with several stiles and gates, walking mostly in trees but later enjoying fine views westwards. Then, on top of

---

WHAT TO LOOK OUT FOR

Take a good look at Abberley Hall's exceptionally tall clock tower. Built by John Joseph Jones in memory of his father, for whom Abberley Hall itself (all Italianate) was built in 1846, it has an octagonal top section before the spire. You may see some deer in a field just beyond it too.

WHERE TO EAT AND DRINK

The Hundred House Hotel was once a collecting centre for tithes from the local area's districts or 'hundreds'. Today's hotel has an enclosed beer garden to the side and an extensive menu. Children are welcome but dogs are only allowed in the garden. On Walk 19 The Manor Arms at Abberley has a roadside terrace.

Walsgrove Hill, you'll see the elaborate and magnificent clock tower (1883) of Abberley Hall. (Move right to see the geese again!) Now go steeply down this meadow, to take a stile into a lane. Turn right to the B4203.

4 Cross carefully. Turn left, along the verge. Take the driveway to Abberley Hall School. Leave the driveway as it swings right, keeping this direction close to the clock tower and all the way, on a track, to the A443. Take the road opposite, 'Wynniattes Way', up to the brow of the hill.

5 Turn right. In about 400yds (366m), reach a bright trig point. Walk along the ridge path a further 650yds (594m) to a Worcestershire Way sign at a path junction, just beyond which are four trees growing in a line across the path. (Walk 19 rejoins here.)

6 Take the path down to the right, initially quite steeply then contouring as it veers right, later descending again. Emerge from the woods over a stile to walk down two large fields (admire the clock tower, now to your right), meeting the road beside The Hundred House Hotel.

Abberley Village and Abberley Hill

A detour through Abberley Village and back through hilly woodland.
See map and information panel for Walk 18

DISTANCE 7.75 miles (12.5km)   **MINIMUM TIME** 3hrs 45min
ASCENT/GRADIENT 1,540ft (469m) ▲▲▲   **LEVEL OF DIFFICULTY** +++

WALK 19 DIRECTIONS (Walk 18 option)

At Point **5** on Walk 18 keep on the road, descending steeply for 180yds (165m). Follow the Worcestershire Way fingerpost down many wooden steps. Take a stile out of the woods, and more stiles across meadows down to The Village, Abberley, Point **A**.

The focal point here is the old church, or perhaps the pub opposite. Dedicated to St Michael, only the Norman chancel remains fully intact. A door and sturdy glass panelling divide it from the remainder, now ruins and exposed to the elements. Abberley's 'new' church is dedicated to St Mary. It lies a couple of minutes' walk from the village. Although 13th-century in style, it was built a mere 150 years ago and largely rebuilt after a fire in 1876.

Turn left, then right, passing The Manor Arms at Abberley pub. Walk for 0.25 mile (400m) to a fingerpost after the stream at

Rodge Cottage's driveway. Leave this meadow by a stile, on to a track heading straight for One Acre Cottage. Just before its garage there's a signposted path to the left, past the cottage's garden. Waymarker posts lead across pasture for some 275yds (251m). Veer right after some woodland, gently up, then down to the left-hand corner stile, Point **B**.

Turn left. Just beyond a private, floodlit tennis court turn right, signposted 'Worc Way South'. Now go straight for 750yds (686m). Turn left at the road. On a bend, where the road is widened for a quarry entrance, do not take the steep flight of wooden steps, but go 80yds (73m) further, downhill, to follow a Worcestershire Way marker, Point **C**. Follow this in woodland for 650yds (594m), then slant across one field before climbing Abberley Hill. You may notice that the trees around you – horse chestnuts – are classically coppiced. In one place this ascent is particularly steep, with views to the adjacent deep quarry. Having attained the ridge, follow 'Worcestershire Way', keeping on it for about 0.5 mile (800m) until a T-junction of paths, distinguished by a Worcestershire Way sign on a single post and four trees growing in a line across the path just before it. Rejoin Walk 18 here, Point **6**.

Overleaf: A view from Abberley Hill (Walks 18 and 19)

Battle at Powick Bridge

A walk based on one of Worcestershire's most significant historic landmarks.

WALK 20

DISTANCE 6.5 miles (10.4km)	**MINIMUM TIME** 3hrs

ASCENT/GRADIENT 195ft (59m) ▲▲▲ **LEVEL OF DIFFICULTY** ✦✦✦

PATHS Pastures, field paths, minor lanes, 10 stiles

LANDSCAPE Mostly riverside and gentle slopes

SUGGESTED MAP OS Explorer 204 Worcester & Droitwich Spa

START/FINISH Grid reference: SO 834522

DOG FRIENDLINESS Mostly sheep pastures, but off lead in middle of walk

PARKING Car park, unsigned, beside A449 roundabout near Powick

PUBLIC TOILETS None en route

WALK 20 DIRECTIONS

Powick Bridge is an historic place. Mills have stood here since the 11th century or earlier. The big mill leat, clear on the OS map, was cut in 1291, and great ironworks used the water.

Walk 30yds (27m) towards the former power station's chimney. Turn left, upstream, beside the River Teme. Barely a mile (1.6km) to the east, it meets the Severn – the site of the Battle of Worcester in 1651, which resolved the Civil War that had blighted the country since 1642. Charles I had been executed in 1649. His heir, Charles II, had returned from exile in France to drum up support, primarily among the Scottish army and die-hard Royalists, to overthrow Cromwell's Parliamentary forces. Die hard they did.

After just 200yds (183m), leave the river to go under the bypass. Aim towards a large white house (Ham Hill) but in the far corner of this meadow move right, beside

huge trees perhaps standing in water. Keeping generally about 100yds (91m) from the left-hand field-edge, walk over 0.5 mile (800m). Pass a solitary oak to locate a stile beyond it, beside an enormous dead oak. In the next field go to the top corner by walking right, round two edges. A stile gives into the once busy Lord's Wood. Our route follows a discernible woodlanders' lane.

After 300yds (274m), stiles zig-zag out of Lord's Wood. Soon pass a solitary house, then turn left on the public road. Fork right 30yds (27m) beyond the signs 'Powick' and '30'. A few paces past The Three Nuns pub, take the track. At the first bend take a stile, half right. Walk along two left-hand field-edges. Passing a house, aim for the far right field corner. Along this right-hand field-edge, walk

POWICK BRIDGE

400yds (366m) to reach a broad field entrance on the right, but turn left, aiming for a stile half-way down the block of woodland. Out of the trees, go forward 60yds (55m), striking half-right to a solitary oak smothering a telegraph pole. Go 40yds (37m) further to find (perhaps with difficulty) a footbridge. Skirt right of Elms (farm), picking up its driveway to the A449.

Turn right briefly, then cross this fast road carefully, to go perhaps 350yds (320m) along Ridgeway Farm's driveway to a fingerpost (walk around the hedge end). Walk 220yds (201m) up the left-hand field-edge, then pass into meadow. Edge along this long and narrow pasture, briefly going close to Carey's Brook, later moving to the right-hand field-edge. Go through a kissing gate beside a massive oak, initially slightly uphill, skirting the left-hand field-edge. In a corner take another kissing gate. Just beyond a track junction, a stile beside a rusted gate gives on to a very wide, green lane. Through another gate in 100yds (91m) – not the pylon field – walk along the right-hand field-edge. At a pond turn left. After Broadfields Farm follow its driveway for 400yds (366m) to a cattle grid. Over this, move

immediately down to the right. Walk through then beside young deciduous plantations, then one arable field to the B4424.

Turn right on the pavement for 60yds (55m). Cross to a gate and overgrown stile. Go three-quarters left, across former strawberry fields, for about 0.25 mile (400m), aiming to enter St Peter's churchyard by a metal kissing gate. From the outside, the stonework of different building phases is very noticeable, a mixture of 12th-, 15th- and 18th-century building. In Powick itself, the unknown Edward Elgar led the band at the mental asylum, writing compositions for it too.

The route goes straight past the church door to another kissing gate. Go ahead on a level path (not down to the right); this becomes a service road to the A449. You want 'Public footpath, Bransford' up to the left, but cross using traffic-lights to the right. Pass Severn Trent Water's Powick Hams installation, then take a waymarked path through young woodland on the small escarpment for about 0.25mile (400m). Wooden steps lead down to the flood plain. Strike diagonally right, to the underpass and the car park, but you've not quite finished yet!

Stroll along the old and disappearing road to Powick Bridge (the A449 road bridge itself dates from 1837). Here two plaques, one easily overlooked, commemorate the battles of 1642 and 1651 between Royalists and Parliamentarians. A little further, on the left, is the magnificent former hydro-electric power station, first built as a mill, and on the site of generations of mills before it, now private residences. Return to your car.

Bewdley's Rails and Trails

Take the Severn Valley Railway and walk back through the Wyre Forest.

DISTANCE	8.5 miles (13.7km) MINIMUM TIME 4hrs
ASCENT/GRADIENT	655ft (200m) ▲▲▲ LEVEL OF DIFFICULTY ✛✛✛
PATHS	Forest tracks, field paths, minor lanes, riverside, 8 stiles
LANDSCAPE	Undulating woodland, riverside, small town
SUGGESTED MAP	OS Explorer 218 Wyre Forest & Kidderminster
START	Grid reference: SO 764799 (Arley Station)
FINISH	Grid reference: SO 791753 (Bewdley Station)
DOG FRIENDLINESS	A train ride: yippee! Fun in forest too
PARKING	Severn Valley Railway station, Bewdley (patrons only, limited space)
PUBLIC TOILETS	At station; also Load Street (short-stay) car park in Bewdley

Flooding a market for manufactured goods with imports is not a modern phenomenon – back in the late 19th century, owners of woodland in the Wyre Forest were complaining about cheaper, Continental oak bark eroding their trade. Close to the Industrial Revolution's heartland and a large population, the Wyre Forest had been an important area for the tanning of leather (and for charcoal production, see Walk 13).

Tanning, the transformation of animal hides or skins into stable, non-porous and durable leather, is a long, multi-staged and labour-intensive process. Dead animals rot quickly – once removed from the slaughtered animal, the flesh has to be cured by salting or drying (or both). At the tannery it is washed and/or adequate moisture is reabsorbed. When oak bark was used, skins were left in the tanning vat for anything from two to 90 days. The final 'dressing' stage may involve dyeing, rolling and polishing.

Tannic acid – or tannin – is found in many plants, for example in the fruits of apples and the barks of trees. Tannin levels in trees vary among the species, but oak has the highest concentration, and was therefore the choice among woodlanders supplying tanneries.

By the early 20th century, demand for timber oak had already fallen because of widespread availability of coal for heating and industrial uses, and iron had displaced it as the favoured shipbuilding material, but demand was propped up by the need for oak bark for tanning. Oak bark had to compete with synthetic tanning agents and the use of other, naturally occurring substances such as fish oil (which oxidises on drying, and is the agent used for chamois leather) and mineral-based agents such as chromium sulphate. The introduction of synthetic and cleverly imitative materials reduced the demand for real leather. The tannery in Bewdley was operational until 1928. The centre of Worcester also had a large tannery, called the Three Springs Tannery. Today, oak bark is almost obsolete as a tanning agent.

In Bewdley the Guildhall houses the tourist information centre and the vibrant Bewdley Museum, focusing on traditional crafts, such as coopering, basket-making and bark peeling. The museum is laid out along a cobbled alleyway with fascinating indoor and outdoor displays. Among its exhibits are old agricultural machinery, a saw-pit and a working hand pump.

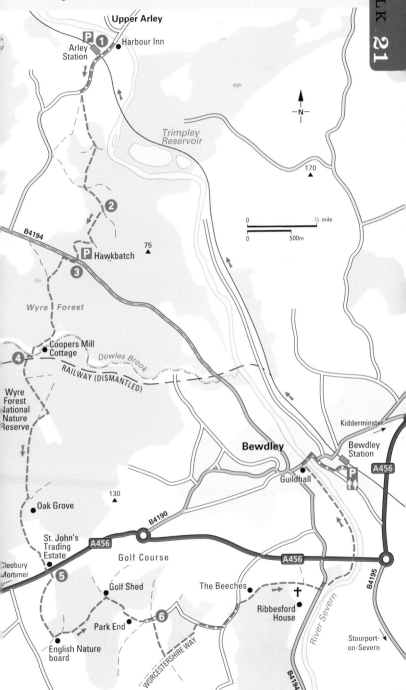

WALK 21 DIRECTIONS

1 From Arley Station go uphill for 700yds (640m). Turn left. After a cottage follow a track into woodland, but soon fork right, ascending (not the driveway of Seckley Cottage). Roughly 30yds (27m) after the pasture on the right ceases, take the left-hand fork, leaving broken trees to your right. Soon bear right. After 500yds (457m), turn left at a track. Just 35yds (32m) on, reach a five-way junction. Go ahead, between posts. In 310yds (230m) reach a fire break with low brick structures.

2 About 40yds (37m) beyond this, turn right down a conifer avenue. After some 440yds (402m), at a red-and-blue post, turn right. At the car park go out to the B4194.

3 Take a few paces right then cross over. Go only 15yds (14m) into the forest and turn right. Before a house turn left (fingerpost), soon joining a better track. (You are in Shropshire but the trees look much the same.) Keep on this for over 0.5 mile (800m), descending on concrete to Dowles Brook's miniature flood plain. Continue for under 0.25 mile (400m), passing Coopers Mill Cottage, then left to a concrete footbridge. Turn immediately right. In 90yds (82m), ascend steeply to an old railway.

4 Go through the gate opposite. After about 600yds (549m) you'll come to a cleared area. Your path is half-right, into oaks (look for a waymarker on a tree stump). Follow this for over 0.5 mile (800m). Skirt a meadow, reaching a gravel track at Oak Grove. Eventually this reaches the A456 beside the St John's Trading Estate.

5 Turn left for 75yds (69m) then turn right (sign, 'Tarn'). Just 30yds (27m) past a 'private garden' sign, take the stile into pasture then another into an abandoned orchard. Instead of taking a third, go perhaps 30yds (27m) further, to another in the corner. Yet another leads into woodland. At a junction, turn left ('English Nature' board). In just 25yds (23m), fork right, descending slightly. Go ahead for 700yds (640m). Near a golf shed turn right. In 240yds (219m), turn two-thirds right. Go past the modern yet small Park End cottage. Turn left, now on tarmac, to a concrete lay-by.

6 Go down a huge field, to a stile just right of a gap in trees. Turn left. Follow this for 500yds (457m) to a road. Turn right for 300yds (274m). Turn left. In 350yds (320m) take the right fork, 'Worcestershire Way'. Avoid The Beeches using stiles. Descend to Ribbesford's church. A horse chestnut avenue leads to the (fast) B4194. Cross first, then turn left for 110yds (100m). Follow the River Severn into Bewdley. Cross Telford's stylish bridge, following signs to the Severn Valley Railway.

Marvels Around Martley

Contemplate the meaning of cider while striding along a marvellous, airy stretch of Worcestershire's countryside.

DISTANCE 7 miles (11.3km)   **MINIMUM TIME** 3hrs 15min

ASCENT/GRADIENT 720ft (219m) ▲▲▲   **LEVEL OF DIFFICULTY** ✦✦✦

PATHS Field paths, lanes, orchard paths, tracks, river meadows, minor roads, 16 stiles

LANDSCAPE Arable, orchards, wooded ridges and Teme Valley

SUGGESTED MAP OS Explorer 204 Worcester & Droitwich Spa

START/FINISH Grid reference: SO 756597

DOG FRIENDLINESS Off-lead opportunities if under control

PARKING St Peter's Church, Martley

PUBLIC TOILETS None en route

Don't believe everything you read in your dictionary. In mine the entry for 'cyder' reads 'Same as cider'. The entry for 'wine' is scarcely less controversial: 'The fermented juice of grapes; a liquor made from other fruits.' If you can accept that grapes are not an essential ingredient of wine, then our 'cyder' is apple wine; if you can't, then it's fermented apple juice. Authentic, old-fashioned cyder is virtually extinct. Some of the smaller manufacturers retain the old word, for example, William Gaymer's Bristol Cyder, and Chevallier's Aspall Suffolk Cyder. The latter contains a heady 7 per cent alcohol by volume, but Weston's Special Vintage Cider Reserve is a dizzying 8.2 per cent.

Mrs Beeton

While being no real authority on drink, Mrs Beeton, writing in my grandmother's inter-war edition of Mrs Beeton's Family Cookery, gives a recipe for cider in which there are just two ingredients, cider apples and water, whereas the adjacent page has a recipe for apple wine, which has three ingredients: sugar, water and…cider. In other words, apple wine is 'cider squared' – a twice fermented-out cider. (By the way, the same publication suggests that one of your servants should clean the silver every Friday.) In the cyder-making process some water was added, because firstly a glutinous pulp was unworkable, and secondly even the hard-working enzymes of farm labourers would not maintain sobriety for (say) scything the corn when drinking copious quantities of a heady ferment.

Sickly Water

Cyder was often a safer drink than water as the acids present in the cyder killed off any water-borne diseases. In 1901, when making a critical assessment of the diet of inmates of the Dore Workhouse (see Walk 41), its medical officer wrote: 'Cold water is a sickly thing to have to drink, especially for agricultural people used to cider.' He may not have been implying that anything was wrong with the water, but his comment shows the ubiquitous nature of cider at that time.

Goodbye Cyder, Hello Cider

As you walk through one of Bulmers' orchards, it's mind-boggling to think that the Bulmers brothers began with just one acre (0.4ha) in 1888 (see Walk 40). In fact, nowadays Herefordshire and Worcestershire's orchards only provide part of the Hereford plant's capacity. The company imports apple juice concentrate from France, Normandy in particular.

Modern-day 'cider' has sugar added and it's almost certainly been fizzed up with carbon dioxide. Even the small print on a can of Bulmers (gassy) Strongbow runs 'dry cider with sugars and sweetener' because the 21st-century palate wouldn't like cyder.

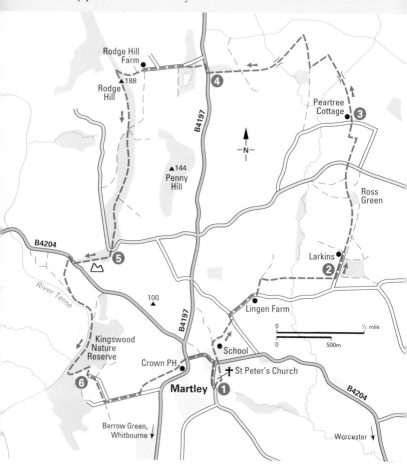

WALK 22 DIRECTIONS

❶ Go up through the churchyard to the B4204. Cross to a rough track. In 100yds (91m) walk in trees, parallel to the school. Turn right into a field, then re-enter the grounds. Briefly follow the left edge of the playing fields, then a gate gives on to a field. At the road, turn left. Turn right, signposted 'Highfields'. Beside Lingen Farm go down a track. At the bend take a stile, straight across the field. Cross a stream, then ascend, taking the right-hand gates. You will then reach a minor road.

WHERE TO EAT AND DRINK

In Martley, the Crown occupies a strategic spot on the homeward stretch. In Berrow Green, 1.25 miles (2km) south, the Admiral Rodney specialises in fish; it has a large beer garden in an elevated position, and a skittles alley. At Knightwick, still on the B4197 but near the A44, is The Talbot with, on site, its own Teme Valley Brewery.

❷ Turn left. At Larkins go ahead, taking two stiles then a field path, not the inviting parallel gravel track. Go ahead for two fields then, at a red sign, don't move right, but forge on, squeezing past a breeze block barn and the driveway of a white bungalow, to walk behind Ross Green's gardens. Cross fields to reach another road. Go straight over, to a partially concealed stile, not diagonally to a prominent fingerpost. Walk beside a barn, then in the next field skirt left to another lane. Turn right for a few paces to a fingerpost pointing into the apple orchard before the defiantly named Peartree Cottage.

❸ Follow waymarkers carefully through this vast young orchard, descending gently. Emerge at a bridge over a ditch, beside apples-sorting equipment. Go 200yds (183m) up this track, to a gap in evergreens. Turn left, down an orchard ride. At a T-junction turn right, up to just before a gate beside a small house. Turn left, almost back on yourself. Go very

WHAT TO LOOK OUT FOR

Martley's red sandstone St Peter's Church claims to have the country's only complete original set of six bells, cast in 1673. It also has some tantalisingly indiscernible medieval wall paintings.

carefully through the orchard, following faded yellow splodges about 1.5ft (45cm) up on the tree trunks, but sometimes obscured by low branches. Leave by a footbridge, crossing fields to the B4197.

❹ Turn right for 60yds (55m). Take an excellent track (mostly tarmac) for 0.5 mile (800m) to Rodge Hill's top. Turn sharp left, 'Worcestershire Way'. Follow this for 1 mile (1.6km). Steps lead down to a road's hairpin bend.

❺ Turn right. In 20yds (18m) turn left, but in only 15yds (14m) turn right again, into conifers. Emerge to drop down steeply. At the B4204 turn right for 30yds (27m). Use a permissive path across two fields to the River Teme. Follow this beautiful riverside walk, later in Kingswood Nature Reserve, for over 0.5 mile (800m). Leave the river when a wire fence requires it. Ascend a path, later a driveway, to a tarmac road.

WHILE YOU'RE THERE

Pay a visit to the Pig Pen (open April to September, usually 2–5pm only), a specialised working farm near Whitbourne. If you have children, they will enjoy trotting around the trail and play areas too.

❻ Turn right, uphill; this soon bends left. Near the brow move right (waymarker) just to walk in the field, not on the road. At the tarmac junction turn left but, in 275yds (251m), walk beside a smart wire fence. Beside fields and allotments, emerge between the Crown and the garage. Pass the telephone box into the village, then turn right to the church and the start of the walk.

Ravenshill Woodland Reserve

Discover a 'mover and shaker' who changed her life and realised a dream.

DISTANCE 2.75 miles (4.4km)   **MINIMUM TIME** 1hr 30min

ASCENT/GRADIENT 475ft (145m) ▲▲   **LEVEL OF DIFFICULTY** +++

PATHS Firm or muddy tracks, meadows, some very short but steep, slippery sections, very little road, 8 stiles

LANDSCAPE Woodlands and rolling green fields

SUGGESTED MAP OS Explorer 204 Worcester & Droitwich Spa

START/FINISH Grid reference: SO 739539

DOG FRIENDLINESS On lead near livestock, off lead in wooded areas (on lead in Nature Reserve, Walk 24)

PARKING Ravenshill Woodland Reserve (donation)

PUBLIC TOILETS At start

You might think that all you need do to set up a woodland reserve is to acquire some land, buy some trees, and persuade some people to help you plant them. It isn't quite as easy as that, a fact attested by the story of Ravenshill Woodland Reserve. Having opted for early retirement from her high-street-name directorship in 1966, Elizabeth Barling set out to do something innovative and completely different. She did have the advantage of starting out with 94 inherited acres (38ha), negotiating the purchase of a little more to round the acreage up to 100 (40ha). However, conservation is a modern concept – most of the land, once ancient woodland, had been stripped of mature trees in 1929, when national stocks of timber were still recovering from the First World War. In 1966 it was a disorderly mass of spindly, regenerated, mixed native species.

The best part of a year was spent living on a houseboat while taking an MSc in Recreation Management at Loughborough University before implementing her ideas. The greatest setback was the loss of her house in the woods, reduced to a large pile of ashes. Ironically, all this destruction occurred one evening while the owner was in Worcester Cathedral enjoying a performance of Haydn's Creation.

Services to Conservation

Look at the suggested map carefully and you will see the word 'Ravenhill' several times, but only once are the birds in the plural, at Ravenshill Wood. In some ways this is an error, but not of the Ordnance Survey's making. A bronze name plate had been ordered, and a rogue 's' had appeared on it; this was pointed out to Miss Barling but she decided to keep the distinction. Later, Ordnance Survey fieldworkers re-mapping the area were shown that 'Ravenshill' was indeed the correct spelling. The information building is rustic and a little ramshackle, but has wall-to-wall wildlife displays, and invites you to borrow wellington boots free of charge. Establishing Ravenshill Woodland Reserve was certainly a labour of love. The full story

RAVENSHILL

is set down in Elizabeth Barling's book, *Birth of a Nature Reserve*, published in 1982. She was recognised with an MBE in 1978 for her services to conservation. Happily, the present owners and the Worcestershire Wildlife Trust have carried forward her philosophy into the reserve's present-day management. The reserve is open daily from April to October and at weekends only from November to March. The distance given in the information panel does not include walking the 0.5 mile (800m) red trail or 1.5 mile (2.4km) blue trail in the reserve itself.

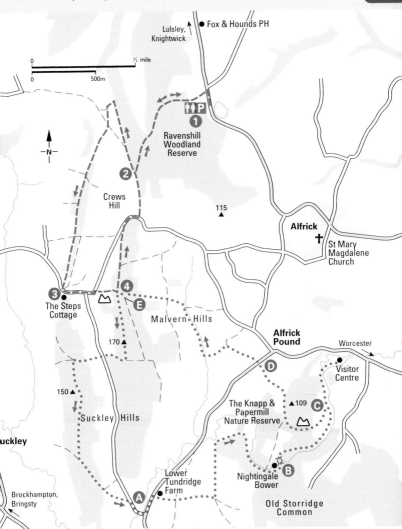

WALK 23 DIRECTIONS

❶ Walk towards Lulsley for roughly 150yds (137m). Turn left on a green track beside Hill Orchard's private drive. Soon

you are in woods. After 300yds (274m) veer left at some wire enclosures. Then 250yds (229m) further, where a stile and nearby gate lead into a field on the right, go just 20yds (18m) further.

69

Now go up to the left on a path. In 120yds (110m) climb a rustic stile and continue ahead. Note well this point, where a path joins obliquely from the left, since you'll be returning this way – the junction is easily missed! Go on for 100yds (91m) to a driveway. Walk for 30yds (27m) away from the house, to follow the sign, 'bridleway', down to the right. Soon, at a line of incongruous laurel bushes, reach the tree-lined Worcestershire Way.

WHERE TO EAT AND DRINK

Less than 0.5 mile (800m) north of the start is the Fox & Hounds in Lulsley, with an enclosed beer garden. Alfrick's post office and stores, in a prime location at the village crossroads, is a vibrant place, generously supplied with fruit. At Knightwick is The Talbot.

2 Turn right. After 650yds (594m) go through a gate. Peel left, hugging the trees for about 350yds (320m) but not going under them. A narrow gap would lead into a second meadow but on the right is a fenced area, guarded by a sinewy field maple. Climb the waymarked stile beside the padlocked gate. After another gate, ascend diagonally right, veering left as it levels. Maintain this line through metal gates across fields, then a wire fence is a handrail to a gate into woodland. Eventually The Steps Cottage comes into view. Reach the road by descending beside a paddock fence, then through little gates.

3 Turn left. Beyond Threshers Barn & Wain House is Crews Court. Here, beside a fingerpost, ascend some wooden steps to a stile. Go left, then immediately right, to ascend a paddock. In trees veer right to take a good stile beside a new-ish metal gate.

Now move 20yds (18m) right to find your path up – here is the old stile, rendered obsolete by the recent fence across its line to the garden gate. Go up quite steeply – perhaps using hands for the last bit up the earth bank, otherwise find a less steep part. Now at the ridge, don't fall off the unexpectedly wobbly stile here.

WHAT TO LOOK OUT FOR

The reservoir opposite Ravenshill Woodland Reserve was dug in 1977. Along Leigh Brook the Worcestershire Wildlife Trust has built suitable holts (otter houses). You'll need patience (and perhaps a sleeping bag) to catch sight of an otter. On Walk 24, Lower Tundridge Farm is a timber-framed building with mullioned and transomed windows. Built in the early 17th century, it was one of the last of its kind, before brick structures became the norm.

4 Turn left. After about 275yds (251m) fork down to the left, not invitingly ahead. At the road, cross it before turning right to walk round the bend. Turn left along the driveway of The Crest, then move left for the Worcestershire Way again. Follow this for 240yds (219m) to Point **2**, then retrace your steps back to the start.

WHILE YOU'RE THERE

Alfrick's Church of St Mary Magdalene is not of extreme architectural interest, but it's extremely pretty – mixed stone facing, a wooden bell tower, and original sandstone window casings. Inside are exposed roof beams and much stained glass of Dutch origin. The Brockhampton Estate draws crowds to its 14th-century, moated manor house and timber-framed gatehouse. Gardeners will appreciate the modest 2.5 acres (1ha) of largely formal grounds at The Garden at The Bannut at Bringsty.

On to the Suckley Hills

This loop takes in a second nature reserve
and more of the Worcestershire Way.
See map and information panel for Walk 23

DISTANCE *4.75 miles (7.7km)* **MINIMUM TIME** *2hrs 30min*
ASCENT/GRADIENT *625ft (190m)* ▲▲▲ **LEVEL OF DIFFICULTY** ✦✦✦

WALK 24 DIRECTIONS
(Walk 23 option)

From Point **4** on Walk 23 turn right on the ridge for 500yds (457m). Turn right, descending to a road. Take the track opposite. Bear right at a junction and, 40yds (37m) beyond, look for an ascending track on the left. Follow this for almost 0.5 mile (800m). Fork left and down. After walking about 250yds (229m) a gate leads through a meadow to a road, Point **A**.

Turn right and, at a T-junction, turn left. Turn right (no sign) beside a long black-and-white building, Lower Tundridge Farm. After 450yds (412m) find a yellow waymarked gatepost. Turn left, along the field-edge. Cross a stile into trees. Soon veer right, not left, to walk beside a wooden fence and a gate back into trees. Atop this muddy slope go right, through a gate, then immediately left – look for a yellow painted arrow on a tree. At Nightingale Bower turn left to cross a new footbridge, Point **B**.

Turn left. At the top turn right. In just 40yds (37m) take a gate back down. Walk beside the brook until a gate at the far end of a meadow, Point **C**. On the right here, through another gate, is a wide, low, grassy footbridge. To see more of The Knapp &

Papermill Nature Reserve and its visitor centre walk on (not over the footbridge) another 500yds (457m), then retrace your steps.

Returning from the visitor centre, go a quarter right (traversing back above your earlier path). In the meadow corner a kissing gate then a narrow opening lead into woods. In 20yds (18m) fork left, soon rising steeply. It emerges after 180yds (165m) at a large, wooden kissing gate, but don't go through it. Turn right. At a T-junction in 80yds (73m) turn left. Within 50yds (46m), at a skew crossing with a lectern-style notice board, go straight on. Join a path from a substantial hut. Soon a good track leads to Alfrick Pound, Point **D**.

Take a fingerpost 20yds (18m) to the left. In the second field veer left, between two large oaks, descending to a gate at a brook. Turn right. Cross two stiles then a third – there are many gates here. Over another stile, turn immediately left, before a massively girthed but broken willow. Round the corner, a stile leads to a meadow. Aim for the right edge of an orchard block, then rise further to take a corner stile into the wood behind it. Go straight up on a path that becomes indistinct to join a good track at Point **E**. Turn right for barely 50yds (46m) to rejoin Walk 23.

Under and Over the Malverns

Take a train to visit Great Malvern,
then return over its attractive backdrop.

DISTANCE 4.5 miles (7.2km) **MINIMUM TIME** 2hrs 30min

ASCENT/GRADIENT 950ft (290m) ▲▲▲ **LEVEL OF DIFFICULTY** ✦✦✦

PATHS Streets, railway bed, woodland paths, one short, steep grassy descent, 3 stiles

LANDSCAPE Suburban, recreational, wooded and pastoral

SUGGESTED MAP OS Explorer 190 Malvern Hills & Bredon Hill

START Grid reference: SO 782457 (Great Malvern Station)

FINISH Grid reference: SO 756424 (Colwall Station)

DOG FRIENDLINESS Few off-lead opportunities, must be controlled on ridge

PARKING Car parks at both railway stations

PUBLIC TOILETS None en route

WALK 25 DIRECTIONS

Out of Great Malvern Station, go ahead and left in 30yds (27m) into Imperial Road (no sign this end).

The presence of spa waters in Malvern had been known for centuries. In 1756, a Dr Wall wrote of the waters' benefits and the 1820s saw the opening of the Baths and Pump Room. The railway in the 1850s brought it to a much wider market. Local architect Edward Wallace Elmslie designed Great Malvern's railway station (1861), considered elegant by the Victorians. Even today the wrought-ironwork of the station's mock pillars (actually drainpipes) are maintained in gaudy colours.

Cross Tiverton Road, turning right on Clarence Road. At the skew junction turn left into Albert Road South. At the end turn left. Beside the railway bridge take a leafy alleyway right, passing extensive new buildings of Malvern College. Cross the next

road, on to Malvern Common. In 600yds (549m), at a dip and just by '60' on the track, pass under the railway. Less than a mile (1.6km) from here, the railway enters Colwall Tunnel.

WHERE TO EAT AND DRINK

On the route, strategically sited near the popular Gardiners Quarry Car Park is The Kettle Sings tea room, and in Colwall, very close to the station, are the Colwall Park Hotel and The Crown Inn at Colwall.

It isn't without reason that the Malvern Hills stand above the Worcestershire Plain. At their centre is a hard rock called pre-Cambrian sienite, flanked by softer red marl and limestone. The people who understood this best were the labourers employed to dig the Colwall Tunnel. Work started in 1856 at both ends, meeting in 1860. While an advance of 5ft (1.5m) per day could be made through the outer rocks, the ancient rock

THE MALVERNS

in Colwall, above the western entrance to the tunnel. During the Second World War the old tunnel was used to store ammunition. The new tunnel's spoil was redeployed in 1959 to provide hard core for the M50 motorway from Strensham to Ross-on-Wye.

The road becomes a green-centred tarmac track, but fork right on to a path before the house ahead. Follow the path for 275yds (251m) gently uphill, to a 'stretched-X' crossing. Keep ahead and level for a further 440yds (402m). At another 'stretched-X', beside an enormous yew (there is a cream-coloured house ahead), take the upward right fork that zig-zags. Very soon, at another green seat, continue straight ahead, gently up. After 275yds (251m) of rising gently, turn right by some rocks and zig-zag gently up to yet another seat. In 175yds (160m), keep straight ahead and up, ignoring a zig-zagging option up left. Dense woodland gives way to bracken and scattered silver birch. After 180yds (165m) ignore a downward right fork. Back into (less dense) woodland, after 140yds (128m) take an acute left turn, finally to meet the ridge path beside some unexpected pines.

Turn left, soon leaving the gravel path to attain the visible top (spot height 357m (1171ft)). Less than 200yds (183m) beyond it, when a path forks right, turn fully right, down a steep ride, zig-zagging to the B4232 at Gardiners Quarry Car Park. Slant right, over tarmac then grass to The Kettle Sings. Turn right, soon keeping ahead on grass to reach a garden fence. Turn left here, over a stile. At a hedgerow move left down a sunken lane, then follow a well waymarked route across fields to Colwall Station.

could slow progress to just a tenth of this. Over its total length of 1,567yds (1,432m) it climbed 58ft (18m). The chief engineer on the project was Stephen Ballard, who, in the previous two decades, had overseen the Hereford and Gloucester Canal (see Walk 27).

As the railway line veers right, keep ahead, moving left to a post box. Across the larger road, follow a fingerpost closely, through trees to a gate, now following a dismantled railway. At wooden steps descend to follow waymarkers across several fairways of the Worcestershire Golf Club on a slightly raised, green track. In dense woodland, turn left – this track leads to the clubhouse and car park. Go diagonally, to the far side of a white building. Cross carefully beside a green, then another fairway, to reach a wide fenced path across fields. A pitted concrete track leads to the A449. Cross this, and the upper road, to a steep centre-railed path. At the Y-junction turn left. You are almost over the Colwall Tunnel.

The brick-lined tunnel was so heavily used by steam locomotives that carriages would emerge with fallen lining bricks on their roofs. Modern trains don't use this tunnel but a parallel, broader one, built close enough to the original to use its ventilation shafts by boring linking shafts. Stephen Ballard was buried in his garden

A Short Amble from Mamble

Discover why the Leominster Canal failed to make money for its owners.

DISTANCE 4.25 miles (6.8km)   **MINIMUM TIME** 2hrs 15min

ASCENT/GRADIENT 625ft (190m) ▲▲▲   **LEVEL OF DIFFICULTY** ✦✦✦

PATHS Minor roads, field and woodland paths, 11 stiles

LANDSCAPE Undulating pastoral landscape

SUGGESTED MAP OS Explorer 203 Ludlow

START/FINISH Grid reference: SO 685712

DOG FRIENDLINESS Lead often desirable

PARKING Lay-by (bend in old road) west of Mamble on A456

PUBLIC TOILETS None en route

Crude forms of coal mining were probably first carried out on the land around the small village of Mamble in prehistoric times. Much later, the Blount family lived at Sodington Hall, and the Mamble coal pits were part of their estate.

It may have been the case that mining was a part-time activity for what were primarily farmworkers. The inference drawn from the absence of much housing in the Marl Brook area is that mining was never more than a small-scale activity. Mamble's coal was not of premium quality, but it was adequate for domestic use and non-critical industrial processes such as lime burning. Coal mining continued in the locality until 1972. The last pit to close was the Mole Colliery at Hunthouse, about 1 mile (1.6km) south-east of Mamble. The more modern, deep-mining techniques are the ones that cause least disruption at the surface. It is believed that, having won the coal from a pit, the ancient miners put it into wagons, to be hauled by horse along a rudimentary tramway to the (partially constructed) canal.

The rationale for the Leominster Canal, sanctioned by a 1791 Act of Parliament, was simple enough – provide a terminus for the distribution of coal emerging from the pits around Mamble, and reduce the price of conveying other goods between Leominster (pronounced 'Lemsta') and the River Severn. An advertisement displayed in 1797 proclaimed a cost saving, priced per ton, on this route of 25 per cent, and a 'more speedy conveyance'. Indeed, in 1796 the price of coal at Leominster was halved.

Collapsed Plans

Coal was loaded on to barges at Wharf House (Grid reference: SO 668704). For various reasons, the canal company failed to build nearly all of the remaining eastward section and the unfinished Southnett Tunnel later collapsed. Its position is near Broombank Farm, roughly below Ash Coppice. All manner of constructional defects in this, and in the Rea Aqueduct, were reported by a consulting engineer. The Rea Aqueduct was built mostly of brick and was the largest single span brick acqueduct in the country at that time. It is still standing, but marked merely as 'FB' on the OS map. It's at Grid reference:

MAMBLE

SO 651703 (you need to be committed to find it); presumably it has been inspected recently, but it's a pretty scary sight nevertheless!

Not having the Southnett Tunnel cut off access to essential water from Dumbleton Brook (beyond the tunnel's eastern portal), so the Stocking Pool (Point ❻), a reservoir, was built. The canal was eventually bought by the railway in the late 1850s and wound down.

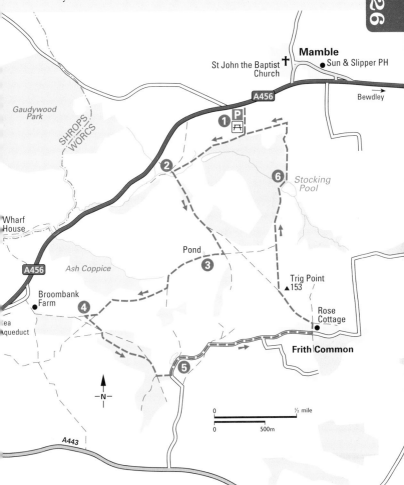

WALK 26 DIRECTIONS

❶ Go to the Tenbury Wells end of the lay-by. Take the gate nearest the road to walk down the left-hand field-edge. At the woodland turn right, shortly entering it by a stile. Go forward at a two-plank bridge. In 200yds (183m) cross pastures to join a cinder track by a white house.

❷ Turn left for 75yds (69m). At a gate move right on a rising woodland track. At a corner stay in woodland, along a broad green path. Fork right shortly before a fence. At this, ascend gently by taking the right fork (waymarker), aiming 50yds (46m) left of a skyline oak. At the top turn right, following the field-edge to a gate beside a small tree-screened pond.

75

3 Keep this line for 250yds (229m) to a stile on the left, shortly before a corner. Climb this but don't follow the waymarker forward and down; instead go through a gate to your right, and continue with this field-edge on your right. In the next one go directly under a large pylon to another stile. Walk initially with the wire fence on your left, but, within 30yds (27m) of the hedgerow beginning, go through a stile, putting this hedgerow on your right. Reach a seven-bar metal gate, one short field before a cherry orchard.

4 Do not go through; instead turn three-quarters around, to go diagonally down this field, in search of a stile (perhaps concealed by a bracken edge) nearly 100yds (91m) left of an old metal gate. Enter an orchard, skirting its right-hand perimeter. Just a few paces around the orchard's bottom corner leave by a stile. Move right a few paces to a wooden post; here fork left (not uphill). In 50yds (46m) go through a small metal gate and see a footbridge down to your left. Across this turn left (waymarker), along a little-used path, to a minor road.

5 Turn left. Keep ahead at a junction, then ascend quite sharply, and drop down past the 'Frith Common' sign. Keep ahead at the next crossroads too. Now you have another pull up, but, before the red telephone box, beside the entrance to Rose

Cottage and The Observatory, take a narrow path. Soon in a field, follow the left-hand edge to a stile. Strike half right (waymarked), descending two pastures easily to walk beside woodland on your left. A gate leads you down to the Stocking Pool.

6 Cross the dam to a gate. Turn left for 350yds (320m), until woodland is also ahead of you. Move right perhaps 40yds (37m) to a stile (not another further right). Over this turn immediately left. In 70yds (64m), cross an avenue diagonally. A waymarker leads you across fields to a gate. Through this return to the car park.

Hereford's Lost Canal

This walk includes a stretch by an abandoned waterway, now being restored.

DISTANCE	7.75 miles (12.5km) MINIMUM TIME 3hrs 30min
ASCENT/GRADIENT	260ft (79m) ▲▲▲ LEVEL OF DIFFICULTY +++
PATHS	Field and woodland paths, minor roads, at least 35 stiles
LANDSCAPE	Gently undulating, mixed farming, woodland, derelict canal
SUGGESTED MAP	OS Explorer 202 Leominster & Bromyard
START/FINISH	Grid reference: SO 642415
DOG FRIENDLINESS	Close control near livestock and on minor roads
PARKING	St Bartholomew's Church, Ashperton
PUBLIC TOILETS	None en route

Unless you know where to look, the only hint of the Hereford and Gloucester Canal in the city of Hereford today is in the street named Canal Road, which led to the canal's western terminus. In the east the canal joined the River Severn at Over, just west of Gloucester. The canal's success was short-lived.

Hereford and Gloucester Canal Trust

Since the 1980s the Hereford and Gloucester Canal Trust has striven to restore the canal to its former glory. The Trust's greatest tangible achievements to date have been restoring the skew bridge at Monkhide, a section of canal at Yarkhill, and the Over Basin, across the border in Gloucestershire. Perhaps the greatest intangible achievement to date has been the partial winning over of opinion. Gradually people in authority have realised that this isn't just men playing with water and boats instead of railways and steam trains (and not just because some of the canal volunteers are women). Perhaps it's because they have noticed the thriving and growing canal leisure sector in adjacent Worcestershire (see Walks 3 and 17), where almost as many people overnight on boats (13 per cent) as they do in bed and breakfast accommodation (14 per cent). A few years ago the planning authorities were successfully lobbied in Hereford city. The service road to a new retail park in the north of the city – connecting Newtown Road and Burcott Road – includes a bridge that spans the course of the old canal, instead of cutting through it or filling it with hardcore or concrete. The Canal Trust is working hand-in-glove with Herefordshire Council to restore a stretch of 350yds (320m) of derelict canal through the newly created Aylestone Park, just north of Hereford's centre.

Ballard's Skew Bridge

Inspired by photographs, I went to see the skew bridge at Monkhide. Do this yourself and, like me, you'll surely be disappointed. True, it's on private land, but no provision has been made for access – in short, you can't legitimately take a good look at engineer Stephen Ballard's mini-masterpiece, now a Grade II listed building. Ballard later worked as a railway engineer (see Walk 25). His grandson, also called Stephen, unveiled a plaque on the bridge. It's a shame that the skew bridge hasn't been made into a modest 'place to visit'.

Not a Bad Deal

Records show that, typically, a lock keeper would be paid 14s per week but his employers would deduct 2s per week for rent. Lock cottages may have been rudimentary, but what could someone today earning, say, £350 per week rent for £50 per week? This brings to mind the old expression, 'the best place to put your money is in bricks and mortar' – house bricks, that is, not canal bricks.

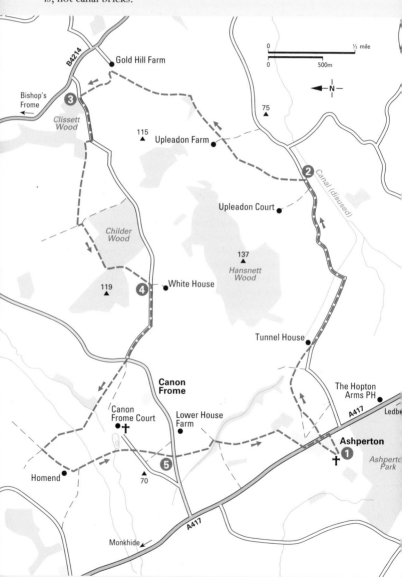

WALK 27 DIRECTIONS

1 From the church car park take the 'forty shillings' gate, behind houses, following waymarkers. Join a track to the A417. Turn left, then right, beside a high wooden fence. Follow a fingerpost across meadows for about 600yds (549m). Find a gate beside a cricket net. Cross the cricket field to a sightscreen, then a track, not joining Haywood Lane (to which the track leads) until some 250yds (229m) further, at the far corner. Turn left, passing Tunnel House. Follow this for roughly 1 mile (1.6km). Find a stile on the left just beyond a gate about 100yds (91m) after the driveway to Upleadon Court.

2 Cross large arable fields and a ditch, then Upleadon Farm's driveway. Aim for the far left-hand corner, taking three gates, then skirt some woodland to your left, striking left (waymarked) at its corner, up a huge field. At Gold Hill Farm go right of a tall shed. Behind this, turn left, over two stiles. Turn right, ascending beside a wooden fence, but from its first corner follow a hawthorn boundary remnant to a road.

3 Turn left for 0.25 mile (400m). Where the road turns left go ahead, initially beside a wood, entering a huge field. Veer slightly left to find a (hidden) handrailed bridge with a broken stile beyond it. Turn left but in 25yds (23m) turn right, before a gate. After 500yds (457m) enter trees. On leaving them strike half right for the large White House.

4 Turn right along the road. When you reach the junction, take the footpath opposite, across a long field. Beyond some trees, aim right of a solitary oak. Walk across fields, over three footbridges and under power lines, passing through a gap to another stile, but do not cross this – note three waymarkers on its far side. Turn left. Just beyond Homend find a stile in a far left-hand corner of an old orchard, shielded by an ash and a larch. Turn left, soon moving right to double gates flanking a wide concrete bridge. After the leafy avenue keep ahead, veering right when a pond is behind trees to your left. Cross the driveway to Canon Frome Court, then another track, finally reaching a road by a spinney.

5 Cross over the road and walk straight to the canal. Turn left. In 140yds (128m) turn right, over the canal. Veer left and uphill, finding a large oak in the top left-hand corner. Keep this line despite the field boundary shortly curving away. On reaching a copse turn right, later moving left into an indistinct lane. The village hall heralds the A417. Turn left, along the pavement. Turn right to the church and the start.

Overleaf: Harvesting cider apples in an apple orchard (Walk 28)

Two Frome Valley Churches

*Secluded churches with unique features,
and special trees amid pastures.*

DISTANCE *4.75 miles (7.7km)*   MINIMUM TIME *2hrs 30min*

ASCENT/GRADIENT *475ft (145m)* ▲▲▲   LEVEL OF DIFFICULTY +++

PATHS *Field paths, dirt tracks, lanes and minor roads, 14 stiles*

LANDSCAPE *Orchards, woodlands and pasture in gently rolling hills*

SUGGESTED MAP *OS Explorer 202 Leominster & Bromyard*

START/FINISH *Grid reference: SO 680502*

DOG FRIENDLINESS *Good early on, but otherwise often among livestock*

PARKING *Roadside just before grassy lane to Acton Beauchamp's church
– please tuck in tightly*

PUBLIC TOILETS *None en route*

At first sight the Church of St Giles at Acton Beauchamp is unremarkable, sitting comfortably on a hillside. Parts of it are Norman, but it was largely rebuilt in 1819. However, if you move to the left of the main door you will see a doorway that leads into the tower. The lintel to this doorway is nothing less than a re-used 9th-century stone sculpture, depicting a bird, a lion, and probably a goat – there is nothing like this from the Anglo-Saxon period in Herefordshire.

Wild Service Trees

Through the gate into the churchyard in Acton Beauchamp, a grassy path slants up to the church. Your eye may follow the shiny black line of the handrail that assists people to and from the church door, but right in front of you is an excellent specimen of a wild service tree. It must have been planted there. Wild service trees actually in the wild are relatively rare nowadays, although it is quite fashionable to plant them in urban settings. Their leaves are easily confused with those of a plane tree, but the latter's bark is very distinctive. It is rare for the seeds of the wild service tree to have the opportunity to germinate since they are eaten and, genetically, destroyed by wasps. (This is in contrast to the consumption of hawthorn berries by birds, for example, where the expulsion of the seed, intact, after digestion of its juicy berry coating, is an effective form of dispersal.)

Academics are uncertain as to the significance of the name 'service'. Most likely it is a contorted Anglicisation of its Latin name *Sorbus torminalis*. Before multiple varieties of apples became available, wild service trees were grown in orchards because their fruits are edible. My dictionary says that a 'sorb' is a wild service tree, and that its fruits are called 'sorb-apples'. (In the southern counties of England they were called chequers.) Other less convincing theories are that 'service' derives from the Latin '*cervisia*' for beer – not far from the contemporary Spanish '*cerveza*' – since the wild service fruits were fermented to make a beery drink, really as a predecessor to cyder. Alternatively, it could have some association with the French word

FROME VALLEY

for cherry, '*cerise*', since, although a kiwi-fruit brown, not red, wild service fruits are of a size and shape comparable to cherries.

In Stanford Bishop, St James' Church is similarly isolated, but has a hilltop position. The stonework is of a similar vintage to that in Acton Beauchamp – Norman and 13th century. Several yew trees dominate the churchyard, the mightiest of which is said to be 1,200 years old; inside, you'll see a certificate to this effect. Also here, nestling in a corner, is the strikingly well preserved, capacious wooden chair said to have been used by St Augustine in the year AD 603.

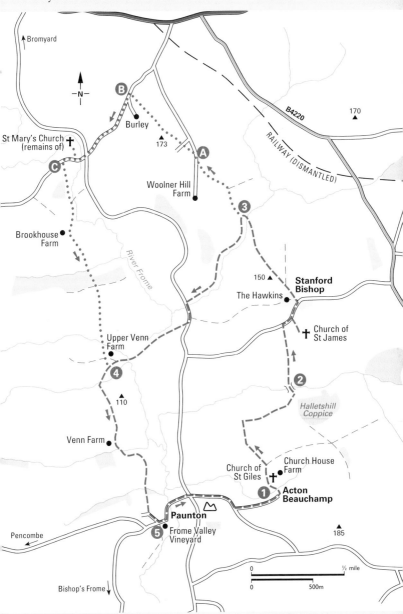

WALK 28 DIRECTIONS

WALK 28

❶ Leave the churchyard by an iron gate in the top corner. Ascend to a stile. Turn left, walking inside the orchard edge. Leave by a stile at the first corner. Contour the next field to a stile then descend slightly to another, hidden stile about 100yds (91m) right of a solitary tree. Turn right, through a gate here, ascending by the field-edge. Keep this line, but, on seeing a gate with a blue waymarker at a protruding corner of Halletshill Coppice, drop straight down, finding wooden steps to a footbridge.

WHAT TO LOOK OUT FOR

As well as orchards, you'll see hop fields and, around Paunton, even vineyards on this walk. They belong to Frome Valley Vineyard. Established in 1992, the product of a modest 4 acres (1.6ha) goes into the making of three dry wines, one medium sweet and a rosé.

❷ Now go straight up the bank. After the trees, keep the hedge on your right to a minor road. Turn right (and visit the church). Return to the road and turn right. At the entrance to The Hawkins take a kissing gate, then follow waymarkers across a track to skirt this farm. Now head down the pastures to a stile with wooden steps. Keep ahead, descending very gently, for 200yds (183m), to cross a footbridge over the Linton Brook. (Walk 29 leaves here.)

WHERE TO EAT AND DRINK

On the B4214 through Bishop's Frome, The Chase Inn has Bulmers' Original, Wye Valley's beer and Frome Valley Vineyard's wine. Dogs are allowed in the garden. Behind it, hidden from the B road, the family-run Green Dragon Inn sells Theakston's and Foster's. Hot drinks and jacket potatoes at Shortwood Family Farm are very reasonably priced.

❸ Turn left, walking beside the Linton Brook for 0.6 mile (1km), to a road. Turn left for 160yds (146m). Turn right. Now the driveway to Upper Venn Farm runs for 0.5 mile (800m). Just before the first shed (Walk 29 rejoins here), turn left to a gate 50yds (46m) along the edge of the field.

❹ Cross the field diagonally, to a gate in the left hedge. Turn left across a field, aiming slightly uphill, beside residual mature oaks. You'll find a stile beyond an electricity pole. Pick up a rough track to Venn Farm, passing alongside its long black barn. Admire the farm's cream walls and exposed timbers, then turn away, along the drive. Follow this down to the minor road.

❺ Turn left, passing Paunton Court (home to the Frome Valley Vineyard) on a sharp bend. At the crossroads go straight over. Climbing this quite steep lane, the Church of St Giles comes into view. Take the first turning on the left to return to your car.

WHILE YOU'RE THERE

Over 300 rose varieties are found at nearby Acton Beauchamp Roses. To the west, south of Pencombe, is the fabulous Shortwood Family Farm, a hands-on livestock experience where younger children will happily spend a whole day. You can join in collecting eggs, feeding the young animals and milking cows and goats. In late October horses work the cider mill. Nearby Bromyard is a 'black-and-white' market town. Don't forget Bishop's Frome's Hop Pocket Craft Centre (see Walk 27).

A Frome Valley Church Ruin

Linger longer in the Frome Valley and visit a creepy ruin.
See map and information panel for Walk 28

DISTANCE 6.25miles (10.1km)   **MINIMUM TIME** 3hrs 15min

ASCENT/GRADIENT 655ft (200m) ▲▲▲   **LEVEL OF DIFFICULTY** ✦✦✦

WALK 29 DIRECTIONS
(Walk 28 option)

At Point **3**, cross the stile, then turn left up the field-edge. Where two stiles span the hedge turn left (waymarked), resuming along the field-edge. At a cluster of gates below a power line go on to the tarmac, Point **A**.

To your left is a cattle grid and driveway to Woolner Hill Farm. Beside it are two gates – take the right-hand one. Use this grassy track for just 25yds (23m), then take the stile on the right here. Go diagonally, crossing a tarmac drive. Waymarkers are initially clear, but in a field with a telegraph pole towards the left corner, veer right to walk beside then through a single line of trees, guided by a single waymarker on a tall post. Pass the building, Burley, some 50yds (46m) to your left. Continue to reach a minor road, Point **B**.

Turn left. Go steadily down this gated road. About 150yds (137m) beyond the crossroads is the decayed avenue leading to the even more decayed church. St Mary's Church appears as a shamefully abandoned ruin. In fact, the church is a Scheduled Ancient Monument and a Category A, Grade II listed building, but it's the usual story

of not enough money to go round. A path leads into an area of graves and tombstones, worthy of a Hammer horror set – you expect one of the tombs to pop open at any moment. Of the church itself, only parts of three contiguous walls and a couple of Norman windows remain.

Back on the lane, go 80yds (73m) further to a stile on the left, Point **C**. Skirt round the plantation of primarily ash trees. Join the driveway to Brookhouse Farm, then bespoke yellow arrows guide you through it. Walk beside an orchard. Look for a wooden handrail and footbridge within 200yds (183m), switching the field boundary to your right. After 400yds (366m), having ascended through trees, keep pretty straight for a good 0.25 mile (400m). Pass in between the tall sheds of Upper Venn Farm. Do not start down the driveway but rejoin Walk 28.

Woolhope and Sollers Hope

A down-and-round-and-up walk in a peaceful farming area.

DISTANCE 6 miles (9.7km)	MINIMUM TIME 2hrs 45min
ASCENT/GRADIENT 525ft (160m) ▲▲▲	LEVEL OF DIFFICULTY ✦✦✦
PATHS Country lanes, woodland tracks and fields, 17 stiles	
LANDSCAPE Hilly, with agriculture and woodland, extensive views	
SUGGESTED MAP OS Explorer 189 Hereford & Ross-on-Wye	
START/FINISH Grid reference: SO 630346	
DOG FRIENDLINESS An exciting stretch, but limited off-lead opportunities	
PARKING Marcle Ridge Picnic Place	
PUBLIC TOILETS None en route	

WALK 30 DIRECTIONS

Begin downhill, along a narrow lane, for about 500yds (457m). On the right along here is some commercial woodland. A fingerpost at a pair of wooden gates points right, swinging down to a wood and a large barn. Note how calcareous the ground is.

Geologically, the so-called Woolhope Dome is a 'denuded anticline', that is, a massive fold of limestone that has been subsequently worn away. Shallow soils make farming only the lower slopes practicable, leaving limestone-loving species to populate the ridges.

Pass the barn and turn left to reach Hyde Farm within 300yds (274m). Veer right but, within 60yds (55m), find a track going steeply uphill and back to your right.

Archaeologists believe that the number of lives lost in the 14th-century to the Black Death may have been exacerbated by food shortages in the two decades that preceded it: the summers, though hot, were short, lowering yields. The 'solution' was to increase the cultivated land by clearing further up the hillsides. Thus some 'ancient woodland' may only date from the post-Black Death period.

Where this woodland track bends left, go straight, over a stile. Cross most of an expansive field, finally turning half left and up, aiming for an aperture in the corner – a track into Busland Wood. On your right are 20th-century larches, but the latter part of the wood, an indigenous deciduous mix, has been coppiced for generations. Walk for 200yds (183m) in this wood, again going straight, into a meadow, where the track turns. Go ahead for 250yds (229m). Find

WHILE YOU'RE THERE

Newbridge Farm Park at Little Marcle has tractor rides, pony rides, handling of the smaller animals, a large outdoor play area and a play barn. At Much Marcle is Weston's Cider (visitor centre).

WHERE TO EAT AND DRINK

Before Woolhope is the Butchers Arms. In Woolhope, The Crown Inn serves Weston's Cider, Wye Valley Fine Ales and good food.

a marker post above a small, dry valley. Swing left, to a gate into more trees. Keep on this track, steadily downhill, for about 0.5 mile (800m), to a tarmac lane – the Butchers Arms is just here. Turn left, up through downtown Woolhope. Just beyond a high wall find a fingerpost on the left. Cross two meadows, then, in the third, find a stile in a dip to the right and go over it. Now see and cross a stiled footbridge. Over this go straight ahead (not right) for about 50yds (46m), then cross a narrow lane. Cross a large field to join a lane at a corner gate. Keep ahead, signed 'Alford's Mill Cottage'. Beyond this, take a stile beside a gate and cross one field. Turn left, over a footbridge. Follow the right-hand field-edge for 130yds (119m). Turn right, over a stile. Keep this line for 0.5 mile (800m), later squeezing between two spinneys into lush pasture. A stile to the right of Court Farm soon leads to St Michael's Church at Sollers Hope.

Built in the English Gothic style, St Michael's Church was altered in 1887, when plaster was removed to reveal the well-preserved timbers of its barrelled roof. Also discovered was a 13th-century stone coffin lid, showing the coat of arms of the de Solers family, who owned the estate and gave the hamlet its name.

Take a stile near the main churchyard entrance to walk to the right of several modern farm buildings. Keep this direction past

an orchard and across another meadow to a stone barn. Cross the lane here to walk beside a ponded stream. Maintain this line, later rising to reach another minor lane. Turn left. One bend after a stream, don't swing right on a private gravel driveway; instead go straight on, signed 'Greyhill Barn', up a rough track beside Lyndalls Wood. Towards the top of the wood and just inside it are the remains of lime kilns. Locally quarried limestone was burnt with coppiced wood (or perhaps coal from the Forest of Dean). The oxidised product, lime, has various uses, such as making whitewash. Ascend for 0.5 mile (800m). Shortly before the brow turn left, up some wooden steps.

To view Oldbury fort, turn right here then retrace your steps. The first 'hedgerow' you come

WHAT TO LOOK OUT FOR

Court Farm in Sollers Hope is nearly 400 years old. As you approach, you'll see an incredibly leaning chimney pot. A little further on, you'll see that it is, indeed, not credible – it's braced with an iron strut in the roof.

to is an earthwork delineating Oldbury's northern boundary. Some people believe that while forts such as Oldbury functioned as defensive focal points in times of need, they were built to some extent for 'show', giving its people a cultural identity, not dissimilar to the Christian 'culture' of building churches.

Having gone up the wooden steps, soon take a gate to put the hedge on your right. Go straight along the ridge for nearly 1.25 miles (2km), passing the radio and television mast. Finally, steep wooden steps lead down to the car park.

Berrington Court: 'Back to The Fruiture'

A moderate stroll around a rural backwater,
among more trees than a forest.

DISTANCE 5.75 miles (9.2km)   MINIMUM TIME 2hrs 30min

ASCENT/GRADIENT 280ft (85m) ▲▲▲   LEVEL OF DIFFICULTY +++

PATHS Town streets, field paths, minor lanes, 15 stiles

LANDSCAPE Undulating mixed farmland, small market town

SUGGESTED MAP OS Explorer 203 Ludlow

START/FINISH Grid reference: SO 598682

DOG FRIENDLINESS Lead preferable most of time

PARKING Long-stay car park, beside swimming pool, Tenbury Wells

PUBLIC TOILETS Off Teme Street and on Market Street

The 'Wells' in Tenbury Wells only came about after attempts in the mid- to late 19th century to capitalise on the mineral water in the town's wells. The Pump Rooms, built in 1862 and recently restored, are its other legacy, but it was too late into the fashion – Malvern Wells, Droitwich Spa, Buxton Spa and the like – for it to yield prolonged success.

Apples Under Threat

Once upon a time Tenbury was known as 'the town in the orchard'. It has been estimated that between 1970 and 1997, 64 per cent of Britain's orchards were grubbed up. Why? Often it was because the grants system operated by the then Ministry of Agriculture, Fisheries and Food (MAFF) encouraged many farmers to grow cereals, not top fruit. Orchards on urban peripheries were, and those that remain still are, ripe for house-building. The cider industry is still thriving – witness the number of young orchards you may see while driving in the two counties – but some varieties of apple are verging on extinction.

Fruit Tree Kits

On this walk you will notice that Frank P Matthews grows a lot of trees. The company sells about 60 varieties of apples. They also have a commercial interest in 'tree heritage', being the supplier of rare species to the Fruit Tree Kits scheme, administered by the Herefordshire Council Parks, Countryside and Leisure Development Service and run every autumn.

The scheme's stated aim is 'to help people source old apple varieties that were once traditionally grown in Herefordshire but that are now rarely planted or difficult to obtain commercially and in turn restore or replant traditional standard orchards.' Those available may be culinary, dessert, or cider apples. Different varieties are available in October each year. A particularly quirky apple is called Ten Commandments; this is a rather insipid dessert apple, in fact, but its strange name comes from its bizarre internal colouring – when cut open, ten red spots are evenly spaced around its core. The Fruit Tree Kits scheme is not exclusively for apples, embracing particular varieties of quince, plum, pear and hazelnut.

TENBURY WELLS

Commercially, apple trees are propagated by grafting on to another rootstock. One reason for this is that they might otherwise grow into large but relatively unproductive trees. The time of maturing, the 'cropping capacity' and the final height of the tree are therefore determined by the rootstock on to which it is grafted. The fruit tree kits for orchards are supplied on rootstock coded 'M25', that is a vigorous sapling that will grow to a standard height of perhaps 33ft (10m). However, to widen the net of propagation, fruit tree kits can also be purchased for growing in a garden. Trees for this purpose are 'M26, dwarfing', growing to 8–12ft (2.4–3.6m) tall, making them practical for the gardener to harvest.

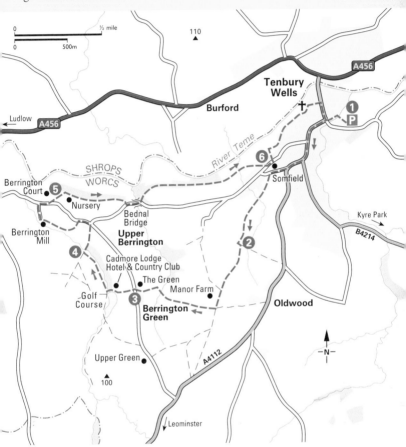

WALK 31 DIRECTIONS

❶ Leave the car park by the 'no exit' sign (for cars!). Over the bridge with railings turn left. At The Crow Hotel, turn right then immediately left. Now walk through Tenbury Wells. Cross over beyond the black-and-white pub, Pembroke House,

follow Oldwood Road but soon take 'Berrington'. After 200yds (183m), before a new house and opposite the bungalow, Somfield, cross a stile. Go half right to another, walk on level ground, following power poles. Cross a ditch over planks and rubble behind fallen trees. Go to the top left corner of a long field.

2 Turn left then right. Cross fields to join the driveway of Manor Farm. About 40yds (37m) beyond the bridge here turn right at a triple waymarker to a close stile. Cross fields for 440yds (402m). Veer down and right, through a rusty gate, then back up left, and through The Green's several gates.

WHERE TO EAT AND DRINK

There are plenty of options in Tenbury Wells, including a pizza house and Kus Kus (a café bar). In the heart of Tenbury are The Crow, which has a beer garden, and The Ship Inn. On the route out you pass Pembroke House, which serves Caffrey's Irish Ale.

3 Take the footpath directly opposite, down a small, tussocky pasture. At the lakeside turn right, passing the Cadmore Lodge Hotel & Country Club. In the car park's far left corner cross a bridge beside a thatched mill house. Turn right along a gravel track, passing new log cabins; within 400yds (366m) reach a junction.

4 Turn right. Perhaps 50yds (46m) before farm buildings fork right (waymarker) to an (overgrown) handrail up to a garden gate. Pass to the right of the house, to a minor road T-junction. Turn left. In 170yds (155m) take the fingerpost, up some steps. Cross this field diagonally. A path leads through bracken to Berrington Mill. Turn right, up the lane, then right to Matthews' tree nursery at Berrington Court.

5 Take the track before a house. Enter the nursery. Walk beside mind-boggling numbers of potted trees under glass (or plastic). Leave this gravel track where it cuts down through woodland. A meadow leads to Bednal Bridge. Just beyond it take double gates into trees. Keep your line when this ample track runs out. Go up an abrupt bank, keeping out of trees. It's now straightforward to the outskirts of Tenbury, guided by yellow waymarkers. Round the backs of gardens, emerge through a gate.

6 Turn left, but only for 20yds (18m). Take a hedge-hugging kissing gate, on the left. In the thistle-wrecked meadow, skirt right for 40yds (37m) to a grass track. Turn left, away from houses, for 40yds (37m) more. Turn right (a gate aperture is now behind you) to hit suburbia again. Turn left. Move left at 'No cycling' sign. Keep on the paved footpath, left of No. 14, soon beside tall garden fences. Emerging at the church, turn left. Opposite a church gate turn right, down Church Walk, to Teme Street and thence your car.

WHAT TO LOOK OUT FOR

No 18 Teme Street (now Kus Kus) once housed Tenbury's most famous resident, yet he lived there for less than a year, struck down by tuberculosis when aged 30. Henry Hill Hickman, born in 1800, was a pioneer of anaesthetics, but never a practitioner (and only recognised posthumously), beyond experimenting with animals.

WHILE YOU'RE THERE

About 3 miles (4.8km) south-east of Tenbury Wells is Kyre Park, a large private house, basically medieval with Elizabethan and Jacobean pieces bolted on. It is set in 32 acres (13ha) of landscaped gardens, with five lakes, a medieval dovecote (resited in 1756), and a brick tithe barn from 1618. For children, there's a 'fun palace' and there's even a miniature soft play area for toddlers. (Open daily, Easter to December.)

The Historic City of Hereford

A walk around a medieval city that still retains some of its ancient charm.

DISTANCE 2.75 miles (4.4km)   MINIMUM TIME 1hr 30min

ASCENT/GRADIENT Negligible ▲▲▲   LEVEL OF DIFFICULTY +++

PATHS City streets, riverside path and tracks

LANDSCAPE Riverside and city

SUGGESTED MAP OS Explorer 189 Hereford & Ross-on-Wye

START/FINISH Grid reference: SO 510403

DOG FRIENDLINESS Not great for dogs, off lead beside river possibly

PARKING Garrick House long-stay, pay-and-display multi-storey car park, Widemarsh Street

PUBLIC TOILETS Blueschool Street, Castle Green, East Street and elsewhere

NOTE Several busy junctions without subways – care needed

The city of Hereford is small enough for market day – Wednesday – to be discernibly busier than other weekdays, though nowadays this is less so since parts of its agricultural economy were slaughtered by the foot and mouth disease episode in 2001. Hereford has a shrinking steel business, and relies heavily on the food industry – Sun Valley (chicken meat products) and Bulmers (cider) – and on you, the visitor. Bulmers went off the rails in 2003, due to what most pundits consider to have been strategic blunders, at one stage seeing its value shrink from £250m to £60m. The company shed several hundred jobs, and was rescued by Scottish & Newcastle (now part of Heineken and Carlsberg). Today neither Sun Valley nor Bulmers employs as many in the city as the Herefordshire Council. The county-corporate logo is a perfect green apple – a conservative choice. The apple may no longer be economically supreme, but it is indubitably more politically correct than a headless chicken – such a choice would certainly have ruffled a few feathers.

History and Architecture

Despite the presence of a munitions factory at Rotherwas, the city was essentially unscathed during the Second World War. Visually, like most other shire towns, Hereford's latter 20th-century development was largely unpleasant – the Inland Revenue building in Broad Street and the encroachment of the Tesco supermarket into the city wall at the Edgar Street roundabout are particular horrors. However, Hereford retains pockets of charm, several of which our route embraces. The city oozes history – its castle site, its cathedral, the Mappa Mundi, and so on. The six-arched Wye Bridge, built in 1490 and strengthened in 1626, has seen a lot of traffic, vehicular and military. It was a focus of fighting in the 1640s, when the city changed hands several times. It has enjoyed relative tranquillity since 1965, when its ugly big sister was built. Beside the Wye Bridge, the Left Bank project – the biggest development since the Maylord Orchards shopping precinct in the 1980s – really made a difference to this quarter of the city, but fell foul of the economic crisis in 2009. Now a large question mark hangs over big plans for the 'redevelopment' of the so-called 'Edgar Street Grid'.

On the walk, take the opportunity to detour south, down Broad Street, to see the tall, honey-and-grey City Library, which also houses the art gallery and museum; currently deemed 'inadequate' for its functions, it was built in a Gothic style, with quite elaborate carvings. Also down here is the refurbished Roman Catholic St Xavier's Church – you can't miss its custard-coloured, Greek Doric columns – threatened with demolition in the 1990s.

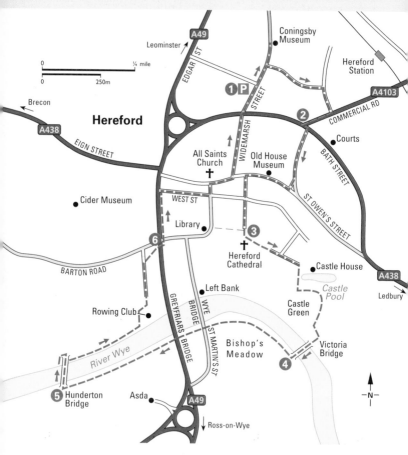

WALK 32 DIRECTIONS

① Turn left out of the car park. Within 150yds (137m) is the Coningsby Hospital built in 1614 (now Coningsby Museum). Go back a little way to walk along industrious Coningsby Street, to a T-junction. Turn right, along Monkmoor Street, noting that Canal Road points to the site of the triple canal basin terminus of the Hereford and Gloucester Canal, now the yard of a builders' merchant. Turn right into Commercial Road, where the Litten Tree occupies a former warehouse. At the Blueschool Street junction on the far side is more city wall, while on the near side are the modern magistrates' courts.

2 Cross first Commercial Road then Bath Street. Follow Union Street, then go right to High Town. Go left down narrow Church Street, to Hereford Cathedral (to the right of which is the tourist information centre).

3 Go left, beside the cathedral, passing the stonemasons' workshop. Go along Castle Street. Shortly before Castle House, a hotel, turn right to Castle Green. Hug the railings on the left, beside Castle Pool (part of the original moat), to walk above the green and its Nelson Column (1809). Zig-zag down to cross Victoria Bridge.

WHILE YOU'RE THERE

Only devout heathens avoid Hereford Cathedral; this, and the Mappa Mundi and Chained Library (entrance fee) are the biggest draws. A circular, three-dimensional model of the hills around Hereford, on the City Library's porch wall, will interest walkers. Mounted on the stair wall is a stunning Roman mosaic floor from nearby Kenchester, and upstairs in the museum you can see bees working in a hive behind only a sheet of glass. On Bishop's Meadow you'll find an endangered species, municipal grass tennis courts – use them or lose them.

WHERE TO EAT AND DRINK

Continental-style 'al fresco piazza lounging' has arrived in Hereford's High Town. The Moka Bar at No. 8 Church Street can be quite a crush – always a good sign. At No. 10 is the Sandwich Bar, and at No. 17 is The Stewing Pot, the Flavours of Herefordshire Restaurant of the Year Winner in 2008. Down tiny Capuchin Yard, off Church Street, is Nutter's, a wholefood coffee shop.

4 Turn right (or left for an extended riverside stroll), passing the putting green, tennis courts and extensive flood defences completed in 2008. Keeping on the south side of the river, cross St Martin's Street to go under Greyfriars Bridge, continuing to Hunderton Bridge.

5 Cross this old railway bridge. Take steps down to head back towards the city. (Walk 40 touches our route here.) Skirt the rowing club, then walk up Greyfriars Avenue. Just before the junction go half right across a car park to go through a pedestrian subway. (But go right, through the car subway, to

see a large chunk of the city wall.) The brick building immediately in front of you is built directly on the city wall. Up some shallow steps, cross St Nicholas' Street with utmost care.

WHAT TO LOOK OUT FOR

Visit the Old House Museum (open Tuesday to Sunday, April to September) in High Town. A three-dimensional model depicts 17th-century Hereford. Near by is the relocated Marchants' House. Near the cathedral, the sign 'Tower open today' means you can climb the cathedral's stairs (most days in school summer holidays).

6 As you begin along Victoria Street, see a solitary tree. A few paces beyond it, about 10ft (3m) up in the city wall, is a hemispherical hollow, supposedly made by a cannon ball embedded there during the siege of Hereford in 1645. (View the cannon ball itself in the museum above the library.) Go along West Street to Broad Street. Turn left. Walk towards All Saints Church – does its tower lean backwards? Turn right then shortly left, down Widemarsh Street, to return to your car.

Beside the River Wye and up Coppet Hill

*This peaceful walk in a popular corner of Herefordshire
includes an energetic climb, rewarded with fine views.*

DISTANCE 6.75 miles (10.9km) **MINIMUM TIME** 2hrs 45min

ASCENT/GRADIENT 855ft (260m) ▲▲▲ **LEVEL OF DIFFICULTY** +++

PATHS Quiet lanes, riverside meadows, woodland paths, 2 stiles

LANDSCAPE Much-photographed river valley

SUGGESTED MAP OS Explorer OL14 Wye Valley & Forest of Dean

START/FINISH Grid reference: SO 575196

DOG FRIENDLINESS Good, but dogs forbidden in castle grounds

PARKING Goodrich Castle pay-and-display car park open daily,
times vary with the season

PUBLIC TOILETS At start

The well-preserved remains of Goodrich Castle seen today are of building work carried out in the 12th and 13th centuries, replacing those from the early 12th century. Some gory traps and ruses kept would-be intruders away. The most often quoted is a tunnel beneath the gate tower that could be blocked by a portcullis; doomed attackers would then be scalded with hot water from above or, better still, burned to death with molten lead (presumably recyclable).

Ghost Story

The castle eventually succumbed to Parliamentarians in 1646 during the Civil War, led by Colonel John Birch, who had successfully attacked the city of Hereford the previous December. The story goes that the colonel's niece, Alice, and Charles Clifford, her lover, fled from the battle, only to meet their deaths trying to cross the River Wye. So watch out for their ghosts on a phantom horse. Goodrich Castle is open daily from 10am to 5pm, except between November and March, when the opening days are Wednesday to Sunday, and the hours are 10am to 1pm and 2pm to 4pm.

A Simple Price

The oddly named Welsh Bicknor was once a detached parish of Monmouthshire. Welsh Bicknor Youth Hostel, a former Victorian rectory, is just one of approximately 225 in England and Wales. The Youth Hostels Association (YHA) began with 73 buildings, many donated, in 1931. The organisation arose to meet the increasing demand from ramblers, cyclists and, in particular, youth organisations for simple, inexpensive accommodation. The YHA has, in relative terms, remained true to this concept, but it has also moved with the times – some would say too slowly, others would say too quickly – improving the quality of its accommodation in line with the relentlessly rising expectations of the recreational public. It seems cherished by the minority that uses it, yet overlooked (inexplicably?) by the majority that doesn't.

COPPET HILL

The YHA was rocked by the closure of the countryside during the 2001 foot and mouth episode. Not only did it lose an estimated £5m in revenue, but individual hostels, run with considerable autonomy, were ineligible for financial assistance as 'small businesses' because of their association with the central organisation – to maintain its cash flow, the YHA had to put ten youth hostels up for sale.

On Location

The area around Symonds Yat has, in recent years, attracted film buffs who wanted to see the locations used for Richard Attenborough's film, *Shadowlands*, the stars of which were Debra Winger, Anthony Hopkins and Symonds Yat. The film was based on the life of C S Lewis, author of *The Chronicles of Narnia*. Coppet Hill Nature Reserve is managed by a trust. It earned Local Nature Reserve status in 2000 after 14 years of conservation management.

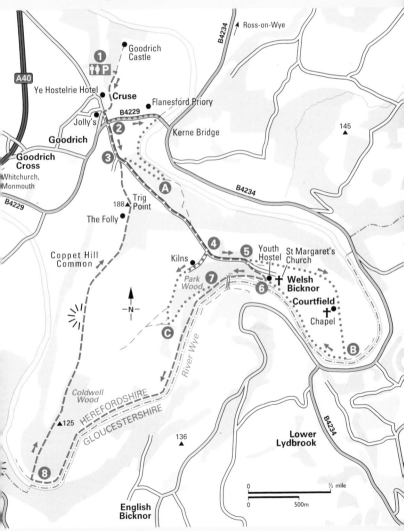

WALK 33 DIRECTIONS

❶ Walk back to the castle access road junction and turn immediately left. In 110yds (100m) cross a bridge over the B4229.

❷ Go up a further 400yds (366m). Ignore another road branching off to the right, but enjoy the view of Kerne Bridge. Opposite, between the two roads, a sign 'Coppet Hill Common' indicates your return route. Go on a few paces – to your left Walk 34 rejoins.

❸ Go another long 0.5 mile (800m) up this dead end, to reach a cattle grid. Here, at the brow, the woods give way to parkland. Go straight ahead for another 325yds (297m) to a solitary horse chestnut tree at a right turn.

❹ Keep ahead for another 400yds (366m), bending left and dipping down, the road once again tree-lined. The road curves right a fraction, while a gravel track goes up a ramp and fractionally left.

❺ Curve right. Ignore the pillared driveway but begin down the youth hostel's driveway. At a welcome sign take a footpath that runs initially parallel to it. Descend wooden steps and a sometimes muddy path to a T-junction beside the River Wye.

❻ Turn right, following the Wye Valley Walk (turn left to visit the church first). In 350yds (320m) you'll reach an old, iron girder railway bridge, which now carries the Wye Valley Walk across the river, but stay this side, passing underneath the bridge. In about 160yds (146m) look carefully for narrow yellow bands of 'rights of way' tape on a tree. (Walk 34 rejoins for the final time here.)

❼ Take the path closest to the river. Continue for about 1.25miles (2km). Enter Coldwell Wood to walk beside the river for a further 0.25 mile (400m). On leaving, keep by the river in preference to a path that follows the woodland's edge. In about 350yds (320m) you'll reach a stile beside a fallen willow.

❽ Turn right, signposted 'Coppet Hill', passing through the line of trees to a stile. Soon begin the arduous woodland ascent. The path levels, later rising to The Folly, then goes down (not up!) to a triangulation point. Follow the clear green sward ahead, becoming a narrow rut then a stepped path, down to the road, close to Point ❸. Retrace your steps to the castle car park.

Around Coppet Hill

*This quirky extension leaves and rejoins the main route
no fewer than three times!*
See map and information panel for Walk 33

DISTANCE *9.75 miles (15.7km)*   **MINIMUM TIME** *4hrs 15min*
ASCENT/GRADIENT *1,215ft (370m)* ▲▲▲   **LEVEL OF DIFFICULTY** +++

WALK 34 DIRECTIONS
(Walk 33 option)

At Point ❷ on Walk 33 descend the bridge's steps to pass Flanesford Priory (little remains of the original 14th-century Augustinian building). After the pavement, walk briefly on the verge to Kerne Bridge (1828). Take steps to a gate on the right. After entering trees, follow the Wye Valley Walk for another 400yds (366m), to a signpost, 'Goodrich 1 mile', Point ❹.

Take this path, emerging near a T-junction, Point ❸. Now follow Walk 33, noting Point ❹ but continuing to Point ❺.

Take the track past a hostile sign indicating footpath only. This hard track is quite straight for 0.5 mile (800m), then curves very gently down, behind Courtfield, a manor house. At a 'Private' sign keep the high wall to your right.

Courtfield Estate belonged to the Catholic Vaughn family, but in 1651 the land was confiscated. It was only in the late 18th century that the majority was returned.

The track ends one field before the River Wye. Descend to the river, Point ❸. Turn right, along the bank, and continue for over 0.5 mile (800m). Just beyond the

YHA's landing stage you'll enter the church grounds.

Although St Margaret's Church combines Norman and Early English styles, it was built as a whole in 1858–9. The ruin beside it, seemingly a farmhouse, contains a decaying cider mill and press.

A few paces past the youth hostel buildings and across its parking area (don't go up the driveway) are wooden steps on the right – this is Point ❻ on Walk 33. Ascend these. At the gate join the driveway, to walk past Point ❺ back to Point ❹. Facing Goodrich, turn left. In 300yds (274m), when new fencing on the left ends, fork left.

After larches and a cattle grid before a new house, fork left, down to gates just beyond overhead cables, Point ❻. Take the left-hand gate, turning sharp left, so passing under the cables again. Continue downhill, along the outside edge of Park Wood. Take a gate into woodland. When 25yds (23m) past a squat stone ruin fork right, to find, within 50yds (46m) a junction of tracks with narrow yellow bands of 'rights of way' tape on a tree – here you rejoin Walk 33 at Point ❼.

97

Kyrle-on-Wye

*An easy perambulation, enjoying the legacy
of a Ross philanthropist.*

WALK 35

DISTANCE *3.25 miles (5.3km)*   MINIMUM TIME *1hr 45min*

ASCENT/GRADIENT *330ft (100m)* ▲▲▲   LEVEL OF DIFFICULTY ✦✦✦

PATHS *Suburban streets, woodland and riverside paths, no stiles*

LANDSCAPE *Classical town built on hill overlooking river*

SUGGESTED MAP *OS Explorer 189 Hereford & Ross-on-Wye
or OL14 Wye Valley & Forest of Dean*

START/FINISH *Grid reference: SO 582239*

DOG FRIENDLINESS *Limited off-lead opportunities*

PARKING *Car park on B4260 between Wilton Bridge and Ross-on-Wye*

PUBLIC TOILETS *In town*

WALK 35 DIRECTIONS

Go to the back of the car park
behind the skate-boarding area
and find a Wye Valley Walk board.
Cross the footbridge to take
the upward path, initially just
slightly left (it's quite steep).
At a junction, turn very sharply
right on a level path, called The
John Kyrle Walk, just a few paces
before a multiple waymarker.

It's as hard to avoid the name John
Kyrle in Ross-on-Wye as it is to
avoid Shakespeare in Stratford-
upon-Avon. Kyrle (1637–1724)
was a wealthy though not overly
rich man. He studied law but
didn't qualify. From his early 20s
he lived a frugal lifestyle, generous
with his money and was the type of
person who 'made things happen'.

WHERE TO EAT AND DRINK

Ross-on-Wye has plenty of
options. On the walk are the
Man of Ross Inn, above the river,
and The Hope & Anchor, beside
the river.

After about 500yds (457m), go
through a gate and descend some
steps to a hollow. Turn left. This
becomes a broader, rough track,
emerging by a house called The
Cleeve. Turn left. At a road go
straight across, continuing on
a path beside houses. Keep on
this alleyway as it crosses several
residential streets, to reach the
disused railway line. Turn left.
Follow this, decorated with trees
and occasional picnic tables, to
near a junction on the B4234.
Cross at the traffic-lights, taking
the gravel path. At the tarmac
turn right (this is Fernbank Road),
ignoring the 'Town and Country
Trail' at the car park opposite.
Keep ahead, not Woodmeadow
Road. Your route becomes a track,
rising steadily alongside Merrivale
Wood Nature Reserve.

Turn left just before the buildings
of Hill Farm, through a gate on
a descending path. After about
30yds (27m) take the larger,
left fork, to soon descend on a
stepped path. At the very bottom
reach a T-junction. Turn right. At

a kissing gate turn left, following a right-hand field-edge. Cross the railway again. An alleyway becomes a cul-de-sac. Turn right into Merrivale Lane but cross immediately to a narrow alleyway beside an electricity sub station. Turn right. Bend left into The Avenue. At its far end turn right, then immediately left into Ashfield Crescent. Next take the first right then, at a skew crossroads, go along Redhill Road. Pass Ashfield Park Avenue and the primary school. Look for a green kissing gate on the right. (Here you are only a few paces from the multiple waymarker on the outward walk.) Through this, skirt the school's playing fields. Two similar gates lead you into the large churchyard. At the wall of The Prospect turn left to enter it through the 1700 gateway. The Prospect is perhaps the most tangible legacy left by John Kyrle – a place for relaxation, and, most important at the time (1696), a fountain providing a ready supply of water to the townsfolk.

Leave The Prospect by the gateway close to St Mary's Church. John Kyrle was buried in the chancel here. Historians have failed to find any blemish upon his character; the nearest thing seems to have been having to go to a petty court for not removing a dung-heap from outside his house – it isn't known whether the horse was his.

Leave the church grounds by the main entrance, passing the fine,

sandstone Rudhall's Almshouses (1575) as you turn left into Church Street. Turn right at a T-junction, to reach the Market Hall and, opposite it on the right, John Kyrle's house. Retrace your steps up High Street, passing the end of Church Street. Stay on High Street until its end. (The tourist information centre is just on the right-hand corner here.) From this junction walk perhaps 70yds (64m) along Wilton Road to see the stone gazebo (formerly Collins' Tower, after its owner), then return to the junction.

The 1830s was a period of great activity in Ross, sparked by the 1830 Improvement Act (which primarily addressed sewage and drainage). The gazebo, together with the nearby Royal Hotel, dates from 1837, when large amounts of the red sandstone were hacked away from the modest cliff to build what is now Wilton Road.

Now pass in front of the Man of Ross Inn (the plaque in front of it describes the 18th-century problems of muddy streets). Descend steps to reach the river across The Hope & Anchor's car park. Turn left. Follow the tarmac path when it turns left. Go diagonally across the grass, crossing the little road to double arches; one is a pedestrian subway – this leads back to the car park.

Overleaf: Ross-on-Wye across the river at dawn (Walk 35)

Aymestrey: Quarrying the Rocks of Ages

What have 'Capability' Brown, Richard Payne Knight and Hanson Aggregates got in common? Find out on this brief walk through time.

DISTANCE *4.75 miles (7.7km)* **MINIMUM TIME** *2hrs 30min*

ASCENT/GRADIENT *525ft (160m)* ▲▲▲ **LEVEL OF DIFFICULTY** ✦✦✦

PATHS *Excellent tracks, field paths, minor roads, steep woodland sections, 11 stiles*

LANDSCAPE *Wooded hills and undulating pastures*

SUGGESTED MAP *OS Explorer 203 Ludlow*

START/FINISH *Grid reference: SO 426658*

DOG FRIENDLINESS *Several opportunities for controlled, off-lead walking; lead needed on two stretches of lane*

PARKING *At old quarry entrance, on east side of A4110, 0.25 mile (400m) north of Aymestrey Bridge*

PUBLIC TOILETS *None en route*

On your way here, you may have seen signs to the village of Shobdon and the adjacent Shobdon Airfield. It was one of the many airfields built in 1940, as part of what was collectively perhaps the biggest civil engineering project undertaken in Britain. At that time a modest, privately owned quarry was operating at Aymestrey. The wartime government used its compulsory purchase powers, ensuring a local supply of stone for the airfield. In its latter years, the quarry was run by Hanson Aggregates.

I don't suppose that anyone at Hanson Aggregates expects, in the fullness of time, to be remembered for their landscape architecture in the same way as the ubiquitous Lancelot 'Capability' Brown, or Richard Payne Knight (see Walk 37), but they should at least be commended for trying.

Landscape Continuum

Unfortunately you will not be best placed to judge the quality of their 'seamless' landscape restoration, since I've primed you to look out for it. Nevertheless, towards the end of the walk, as you descend to the former quarry area, there is little to indicate that the immediate landscape has been recently manufactured, although your curiosity may be alerted by the absence of any really substantial trees. Unlike many quarries, the plan here was not to provide any sort of lake-based recreation, but to return the land to a mixture of agricultural use (sheep grazing, it seems) and woodland.

In geological time, man's quarrying is scarcely a moment. Unfortunately, working out a quarry can take up a fair amount of a person's lifetime – people tend not to like quarries in their backyards, so quarries often get a bad press. The quarry companies will argue that 'restoration' and 'environmental sensitivity' were among their objectives a decade or two before their current fashionability, and that, far more often than not, sand and gravel quarries are returned to a level of agricultural utility that at least equals the one before.

AYMESTREY

Glacial Gorge

West of Aymestrey the River Lugg runs in a small but spectacular gorge. This is a glacial overflow channel that exploited a fault in the rock, associated with the glacial Wigmore Lake. The paucity of contours on the suggested map a few grid squares to the north shows the position of the former lake. At Mortimer's Cross, Richard of York's son Edward defeated the Lancastrian army in 1461 in one of the battles that changed the course of the Wars of the Roses (Edward was crowned King later that year). The battle site is 0.5 mile (800m) south of the road junction named Mortimer's Cross. The cross itself dates from 1799.

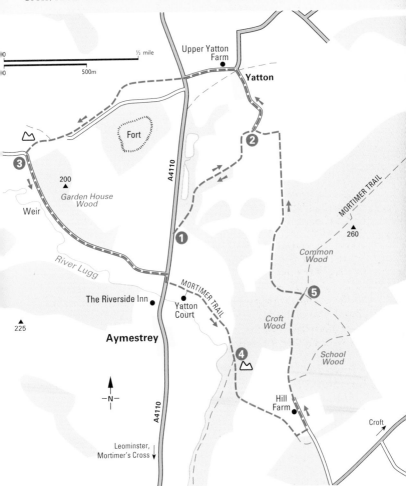

WALK 36 DIRECTIONS

❶ Walk up the access road for 750yds (686m), until just before a junction of tracks. Note a stile on the right – your route returns over this.

❷ Turn left then, in 25yds (23m), curve right, passing a seemingly nameless house with a stone wall relic in its garden. Shortly curve left to walk through Yatton, to a T-junction. Turn left to the A4110. Cross directly to a stile, striking across this field to a gap. In the next field veer left to skirt round the right edge of (not over) an oak and ash embankment, to find a corner stile. Walk up the left edge of this field but, at the brow, where it bends for some 70yds (64m) to a corner, take a stile in the hedge to walk along its other side. Within 60yds (55m) you will be on a clear path, steeply down through woodland, a ravine on your left. Join a rough driveway to a minor road. (The glacial overflow channel is directly ahead.)

WHILE YOU'RE THERE

Visit Mortimer's Cross Water Mill, managed by English Heritage (open Sundays and Bank Holiday Mondays, April to September, 10am-4pm, guided tour at 11am, 1pm and 3pm). Remarkably, this 18th-century mill was still grinding corn commercially in the 1940s. The wheel still turns today from time to time. The Croft Estate has its castle and waymarked walks.

---

③ Turn left here, joining the Mortimer Trail. Enjoy this wooded, riverside lane for nearly 0.75 mile (1.2km), to reach the A4110 again. Cross, then walk for just 25yds (23m) to the right. (The Riverside Inn is about 175yds/160m further.) Take a raised green track, heading for the hills. Then go diagonally across two fields, to a stile and wooden steps.

④ Within a few paces fork left to ascend steeply through the trees. Leave by a stile, to cross two meadows diagonally. Over a double stile, walk along the left-hand edge of a field, still heading downhill. At the trees turn left. Soon reach a tarmac road. Turn left along the road,

---

WHERE TO EAT AND DRINK

At Aymestrey Bridge (over the River Lugg), The Riverside Inn has ales from Stoke Lacy and ciders and perries from Much Marcle and Wigmore. It also boasted the 2007 Herefordshire Young Chef of the Year award. The Mortimer's Cross Inn, at the junction of that name, has a beer garden and a children's play area.

---

now going back uphill. Beyond Hill Farm, enter the Croft Estate. Walk along this hard gravel track. After 110yds (100m), ignore a right fork but, 550yds (503m) further on, you must leave it. This spot is identified where deciduous trees give way to conifers on the left and you see a Mortimer Trail marker post on the wide ride between larches and evergreens on the right.

⑤ Turn left (there is no signpost). Within 110yds (100m) go half right and more steeply down on an aged access track. Within 250yds (229m) look out for a modern wooden gate, waymarked, leading out of the woods. Walk along its right-hand edge, admiring the former quarry's new landscape. Walk briefly in trees then out and, at the far corner, within the field, turn left to Point **②**. Retrace your steps to the start of the walk.

WHAT TO LOOK OUT FOR

There are stunning brick-arched barns at Upper Yatton Farm. These tall stone structures have brick apertures; one is filled in with attractive gridded brickwork. Later, look back from the other side of the A4110 to see more arches.

Picturesque Downton Castle

A long stretch in a landscape designed to please the eye.

DISTANCE 10 miles (16.1km)   MINIMUM TIME 5hrs

ASCENT/GRADIENT 1,200ft (366m) ▲▲▲   LEVEL OF DIFFICULTY +++

PATHS Pastures, leafy paths, grass tracks, dirt tracks, tarmac lanes, one steep, earthy bank, 13 stiles

LANDSCAPE Rolling country, wooded and farmed, above River Teme

SUGGESTED MAP OS Explorer 203 Ludlow

START/FINISH Grid reference: SO 403741

DOG FRIENDLINESS Mostly on lead, lots of game birds

PARKING Community centre and village hall car park, Leintwardine

PUBLIC TOILETS At start (not always open)

By the end of the 18th century, formal neatness in landscape architecture had fallen from favour; the new word on the lips of those who counted was 'picturesque'. This craving for a '*laissez-faire*' type of landscape had been of great benefit to Ross-on-Wye (see Walk 35), where the Wye Tour had become the must-do trip. Downton on the Rock was to benefit from Richard Payne Knight, under whose direction Downton Castle was built between 1772 and 1778. If you like regimented rows of trees, twee fountains, manicured lawns and symmetrical paths, then it's not the castle for you.

Richard Payne Knight

Richard Payne Knight knew exactly the sort of landscape he wanted for Downton Castle, having travelled extensively, particularly in Italy. He sought a rugged, wild view, like those seen in the landscape paintings of Nicolas Poussin, Claude Lorrain and Salvator Rosa, who had produced their best works in the mid-17th century. Poussin had worked at the Louvre in Paris as painter to the king, whereas Lorrain and Rosa had studied in Naples. None came from privileged backgrounds and all had struggled to gain recognition for their work. For some time after they had established themselves as artists, all three lived as near neighbours in a street in Rome called Trinità dè Monti. It would be interesting to compare their works with those of the little-known English painter, Thomas Hearne, who painted several views of the Downton Estate. Incidentally, the British landscape painter, John Constable, was born in 1776, when Downton Castle was being built. It is said that, when aged about 20, sight of *Hagar and the Angel*, by Claude Lorrain. sparked Constable's smouldering ambition to be an artist.

As for the privately owned Downton Castle's interior, it is wholly classical in style. Some alterations and additions were made in the 1860s.

Roman Leintwardine

The Romans built a fort beside the River Teme here, and stayed at Leintwardine until the late 4th century AD. Where an early church is found

DOWNTON ON THE ROCK

within a Roman earthwork, the inference is that usage of the site continued when the Romans left, as is the case with Leintwardine. The High Street lies on the line of the Roman Watling Street. Today Leintwardine's population is well below half its late 19th-century figure of nearly 2,000.

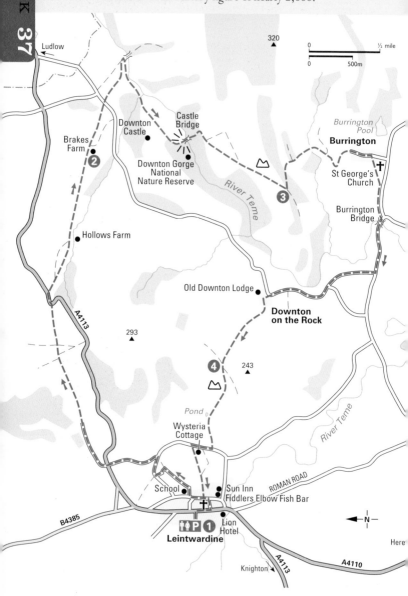

WALK 37 DIRECTIONS

1 Begin downhill, very soon taking the first left, Church Street. Turn left. As you reach the primary school, turn right.

Aim for a brick, brown-and-white house but, after a two-plank footbridge, go left to a tarmac road. Turn right. In 300yds (274m) turn left, to the A4113. Cross, turning immediately right

DOWNTON ON THE ROCK

up a lane. Ascend for a short mile (1.6km). Soon after a skew junction go forward, taking the left of two gates. Just beyond a corrugated shelter, take a stile on the right. Go three-quarters left, across two more fields, to replanted woodland. At the A4113 turn left but soon right, beside a wire fence. At the end follow the field edge round to the left for 40yds (37m). Go down an earthy bank (on your bottom?) in trees to pass stables on your right, then along a good dirt road, soon dead straight for 0.5 mile (800m) to Brakes Farm.

2 Go straight ahead (waymarker). Cross a minor road diagonally, then cross fields to a minor lane beside houses Nos 20 and 19. Turn left. Soon turn right, downhill. Turn right, along the river, just before a bridge over the River Teme. Skirt two unnamed houses. Up a bank, join a dirt road. Follow this to Castle Bridge. Ascend but within 110yds (100m) of leaving woodland go half right, across a field, rejoining the dirt road into forest for perhaps 60yds (55m). (If the footpath is not established, it would make sense to go round the road, not trample the crop.) Scramble up a bank (waymarker). Traverse the steep meadow to a gate in the top, among oaks. Keep this line to go down a wide meadow, locating a stile on the left into harvested trees.

3 Turn left and descend. When you reach open meadow, curve round a dry valley. At a left bend go through a gate on the right. Go left of a specimen oak to a hidden stile in the bottom corner. Cross over a footbridge and turn right. Cross meadow to a gate, and soon reach a minor road. Turn right. Descend easily through Burrington, to St George's

WHAT TO LOOK OUT FOR

At St George's Church, Burrington, are several iron slab tombstones, among which is that of 'Richard Knight, MDCCXLV' (1745). He was the grandfather of Richard Payne Knight, who had purchased the Downton Estate with money earned from his life as one of the Shropshire ironmasters.

Church. Behind the church, cross meadows to Burrington Bridge. Cross the River Teme. After 650yds (594m) take the right turn. When you reach Downton, head towards Old Downton Lodge, but then turn left. Beyond a wall take the rightmost gate (waymarker), along an old lane. Shortly move right to ascend a right-hand field-edge, soon following a beech-lined avenue to reach a junction with a dirt track.

WHERE TO EAT AND DRINK

There are no refreshments on the way, but in Leintwardine fish and chips are available Tuesdays to Saturdays from the Fiddlers Elbow Fish Bar. Weekend walking groups can phone in advance and have their fish and chips lunch served to them at the Sun Inn, three doors away, washed down with a beer. Leintwardine's Lion Hotel has a riverside beer garden.

4 Over a stile into an expansive field, swing left to descend, initially steeply. Past a small (possibly dry) pond veer left along a right-hand field-edge to a road. Turn right. Within 275yds (251m), at Wisteria Cottage, take a kissing gate. Cross three fields to soon emerge on Watling Street. Turn right to Church Street and back to the start.

WALK 38

Kilpeck and Orcop Hill

*A walk once enjoyed by a young woman
who became a wartime heroine.*

DISTANCE 4.75 miles (7.7km)   MINIMUM TIME 2hrs 15min

ASCENT/GRADIENT 590ft (180m) ▲▲▲   LEVEL OF DIFFICULTY ✦✦✦

PATHS Field paths, tracks and minor lanes, 21 stiles

LANDSCAPE Wooded, grazed and cultivated hills

SUGGESTED MAP OS Explorer 189 Hereford & Ross-on-Wye

START/FINISH Grid reference: SO 445304

DOG FRIENDLINESS Good, on-lead exercise, not allowed in Kilpeck churchyard

PARKING Spaces beside St Mary's and St David's Church, Kilpeck

PUBLIC TOILETS None en route

The bottom of a garden seems an odd place for a museum, but the Violette Szabo, GC Museum is a very personal one. It stands in the grounds of Cartref, the modest house to which Violette Szabó would come to visit her cousins. Rosemary Rigby, who lives there now, is both the museum's creator and curator. Among the many attending the museum's opening in 2000 was Violette's daughter, Tania.

Violette Bushell had a French mother and an English father. When Violette was 11, they moved to London. Violette met Etienne Szabó, a Hungarian-born French national 12 years older than she, at London's Bastille Day Parade in 1940. After a whirlwind romance – not uncommon in wartime – they married 41 days later. In February 1942, Violette gave birth to Tania, whom Etienne was never to see, for he succumbed to chest wounds inflicted in the Battle of El Alamein that October. Seeking revenge, Violette joined the Auxillery Territorial Service (ATS), from where she was head-hunted by the French section of the Special Operations Executive (SOE). Her second mission on the ground in France was to be her last.

Among the museum's exhibits is a door of the car believed to have been the one in which Violette Szabó, Jacques Dufour (the local Maquis leader) and a friend of his had been travelling to visit another Maquis member when they encountered a Nazi road block. In the ensuing gun battle her two companions escaped, uninjured, but Violette had to surrender when she ran out of ammunition. She was – posthumously – awarded the George Cross, the first woman to be honoured in this way. Although unaware of major Nazi troop movements, it isn't clear why Dufour, who was driving, decided to take on the soldiers at the road block, rather than turning the car round and hoping they wouldn't be pursued, or at least hoping to find a better escape route, for example, but this was the beginning of the end.

From her capture on 10 June 1944 until her execution on 28 January 1945, Violette was moved eight times, enduring rape, brutal assaults and inhumane living conditions, particularly at Ravensbrück concentration camp and three months at Königsberg on the Russian Front. The outcome could have been so different. Alerted to where Violette was being held, two

KILPECK

SOE colleagues intended to rescue her from Limoges Prison, which wasn't heavily guarded. Tragically, just hours before they planned to do it, she was moved to Fresnes Prison in Paris.

Of the SOE's 55 women members, 11 were killed in service, either in France or in concentration camps. R J Minney's biography of Violette Szabó was published in 1956. In the 1958 film, *Carve Her Name with Pride*, Virginia McKenna – who attended the museum's opening – portrayed Violette. Although Steve Tomlinson's summary account of Violette Szabó's life, available at the museum, doesn't dwell on Ravensbrück's horrors (where 92,000 women died), it still leaves a grim memory of a fanatically and remorselessly cruel regime.

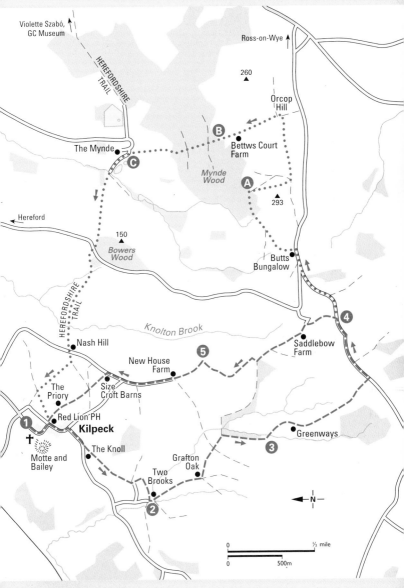

WALK 38 DIRECTIONS

❶ Walk down to the Red Lion, turn right and at the junction, follow 'Garway Hill'. Take the second fingerpost to hug the hedge just behind The Knoll (house). Move right, to stand beside the stile from The Knoll's garden. Aim for the left side of a white house three fields away. Cross on to this lane, immediately turn left and follow waymarkers through trees. Go straight down a field to near a junction.

❷ Turn left, past Two Brooks. After 500yds (457m) turn left, through a gate by Grafton Oak, tucked behind. Soon in a scenic meadow, follow the fence until a crossing stile. Now keep ahead but drift down, guided by a gigantic oak. The stile you need is ahead, not another, further down, that crosses a brook. Contour with trees on your left for two fields. In the third find a footbridge down and left.

❸ Follow waymarkers, diagonally up the field. Walk with a wire fence on your right. Leave this long field at its top end (but, oddly, the waymarked route seems intrusive, crossing and re-crossing

the wire fence on your right near Greenways, via a wooded area). Go up but leftish to an opening beside a hollow oak. Move left to walk along the left-hand field-edge. Ignore a waymarker into the left-hand field – any way out has completely disappeared. Instead keep straight, to a tarmac road. Turn left. After 650yds (594m) a fingerpost slants left. (Walk 39 starts here.)

❹ Take this path through bracken to a track. Turn right for 25yds (23m), then left, to pass to the right of Saddlebow Farm. The avenue below leads into a field. Walk along this right edge, to just before another gate. Join a very good track, following it for 650yds (594m), to three gates in a corner.

❺ Take the second on the left. Beyond New House Farm go over 0.25 mile (400m) to a junction. Don't turn down to Kilpeck yet! Go 160yds (146m) further. Go left just beyond Size Croft Barns. Descend to an unseen gap 120yds (110m) right of the bottom left-hand corner. Out of this copse, cross two fields to pass between the buildings of The Priory. An avenue of horse chestnuts leads to the Red Lion.

Orcop Hill – a Longer Walk

Enjoy the views for longer, with an opportunity to go on foot to the Violette Szabó, GC Museum (see While You're There).

See map and information panel for Walk 38

DISTANCE *7 miles (11.3km)*   MINIMUM TIME *3hrs 30min*

ASCENT/GRADIENT *950ft (290m)* ▲▲▲   LEVEL OF DIFFICULTY +++

WALK 39 DIRECTIONS (Walk 38 option)

From Point ❹ on Walk 38 keep on the road for nearly 0.5 mile (800m). Beside Butts Bungalow, take a delightful track to Mynde Wood. Fork right to ascend gently. After 300yds (274m) in the woods find a waymarked double stile, Point ❹.

The next stile to negotiate is 400yds (366m) away, well left of the line of the steepest slope. Turn left on to a green motorway. At the T-junction turn left on tarmac. Over the crest, drop steeply but only half-way: a stile just after a grassy cattle grid enables you to skirt Bettws Court Farm. Re-ascend. About 60yds (55m) beyond a protruding corner take a stile into Mynde Wood once more, Point ❸.

Descend steadily, crossing several tracks. Leave the wood for a paddock. Go right of the brick-floored stables to a track, then turn left, beside a house. Through the gate ahead, turn right. Temporary fencing for horses makes the way unclear. You can use the next gate ahead, then go right, into and out of the rusty-red corrugated shed (which garages an old fire engine), take a gate on the left and turn right. Standing on a tarmac road, with The Mynde to your right and two ponds to your left, you are at Point ❸.

From the outside The Mynde is imposing yet bland, its rendered finish detracting from any embellishments. Inside, it apparently has a very large hall, but none of the privately owned building, in part 16th century, is open to the public.

Just past the ponds, fork left, following a dirt track for over 0.5 mile (800m). Just before the minor road it bends right – go straight on, hugging the left field edge, to pass a modern house to your right. Cross this road and the next field. At a woody corner go down, left, to cross a stream. Now go two-thirds right and only a little up to a narrow metal gate. Strike across this large field, neither gaining nor losing height for the first 200yds (183m) then, veering left a fraction, descend steadily to cross a stream. Go up again, to reach a minor road beside the cottage, Nash Hill. Cross this and into another field. Go diagonally for 60yds (55m) then straight down the slope for two fields. At a ditch, go left, to cross two more fields and emerge in the village of Kilpeck beside the Red Lion public house.

Hereford's Percy and Fred

*Catch a bus from Hereford for this linear
walk beside orchards and the Wye.*

DISTANCE *3.75 miles (6km)*   MINIMUM TIME *1hr 45min*

ASCENT/GRADIENT *82ft (25m)* ▲▲▲   LEVEL OF DIFFICULTY ✦✦✦

PATHS *Farmland and woodland paths, old railway bed, 3 stiles*

LANDSCAPE *Orchards, arable fields and riverside pastures*

SUGGESTED MAP *OS Explorer 189 Hereford & Ross-on-Wye*

START *Grid reference: SO 471414 (city bus stop SO 503401)*

FINISH *Grid reference: SO 503400 (Cider Museum)*

DOG FRIENDLINESS *Some arable fields, but many cattle beside Wye*

PARKING *At Cider Museum (patrons only); or city centre*

PUBLIC TOILETS *None en route but several in city*

NOTE *Catch 71 or 71A bus (hourly) from nearby Eign Street (shown on map
for Walk 32) towards Credenhill and ask for Wyevale Nurseries*

WALK 40 DIRECTIONS

From the bus stop opposite
Wyevale Nurseries on the King's
Acre Road, take a bridleway
between beech hedges. It's
straight. Eventually cross a farm
track to put a hedge on your left.
At the end of Wyevale Wood,
cross a stile. In adjacent modern
orchards one substantial oak
stands defiantly.

By the time you reach these
orchards the bus you caught
will be in Credenhill, home of
the founding brothers of H P
Bulmers, Percy and Fred. Their
father was rector at Credenhill
for several decades, and was also
a contributor to the *Herefordshire
Pomona*, a tome on apples. In
1887, having completed a history
degree at Cambridge, Fred
joined his brother in preference
to taking up the opportunity to
tutor the King of Siam's sons.
It was some time before steam
power eased the physical effort

of cider-making. At the start,
both brothers worked a 16-hour
day for much of the year, either
walking the 4 miles (6.4km) home
to save the rail fare or sleeping
overnight at their workplace. On
the latter occasions, the suppers
their mother had cooked for them
would be taken by a boy on the
train from Credenhill to Hereford.

Keep ahead, then cross a tarmac
road. Keep on this line with a
hedge on your left, eventually to
reach, in a corner, a kissing gate
(Wye Valley Walk marker). Sheep
graze in the traditional orchard
on the left. Within 60yds (55m),
cross another road at Breinton

WHILE YOU'RE THERE

Visit the Cider Museum or
the child-friendly Waterworks
Museum which combines the
history of drinking water with
the engineering of Victorian
steam pumping engines (check
for opening times). For more
ideas see Walk 32.

Court Lodge. Go diagonally across an old orchard then beside a tennis court to a kissing gate. Here head straight across another old orchard, not right (leaving the Wye Valley Walk). Under some power lines cross a new-ish fence. Keep this diagonal to a green path that passes to the right of the churchyard, reaching a kissing gate. Atop a wooded embankment, initially skirting the vicarage's vast garden, walk beside more grazed orchards.

The Bulmer brothers' business stuttered early on when the local apple crop was so poor that they had to buy their raw material expensively from Somerset. The turning point came when, having filled new, large storage tanks with cider in a year of good harvest, they were able to sell all their stocks at a premium price after a bad harvest two years later.

Direct or 'junk' mail is not a new concept. Bulmers were one of the earliest to apply this method of creating demand. The brothers would spend their evenings poring over directories, to cull names and addresses of landed gentry, peers, the clergy and doctors, then send out circulars to this 'target audience'. According to Fred's account, this effort meant that after some years they had accrued 20,000 customers, a big enough base for them to become a 'wholesale only' company. Bulmers' Woodpecker brand was first sold in 1896. (For modern-day Bulmers see Walk 32.)

Beyond these orchards a kissing gate leads into an open field. Soon look for another metal kissing gate that puts the hedge on your left, in pasture. Some 60yds (55m) beyond a massive plane tree, turn right to cross a stile down to the

River Wye. Turn left. Walk for 1.5 miles (2.4km), to the old railway bridge.

As a child, Fred Bulmer suffered so badly from asthma that he did not go to school. During this school-less childhood he taught himself French. When the business blossomed he went on a visit to France, where the cider-makers of Epernay gave him advice and colleagues demonstrated their *méthode champagnoise*.

First published in 1937, and written in the style of the period, *Early Days of Cider Making* by Edward Frederick Bulmer is a delightful read, a story of sweat, endeavour, opportunism and good fortune. It's available from the Cider Museum.

At the old railway bridge, ascend steps to turn left – beware of cyclists. Go along this old railway trackbed. Just under a road bridge, fork left: this sylvan cyclepath and walkway spills into Retail Britain. Cross Sainsbury's car park to find, beyond the Travelodge, the Cider Museum.

The Delights of Abbey Dore

In search of a 19th-century workhouse in the glorious Golden Valley.

> DISTANCE 8 miles (12.9km)   MINIMUM TIME 3hrs 45min
>
> ASCENT/GRADIENT 540ft (165m) ▲▲▲   LEVEL OF DIFFICULTY ✦✦✦
>
> PATHS Meadows, tracks and woodland paths (one stony, awkward descent), 22 stiles
>
> LANDSCAPE Quintessential Herefordshire
>
> SUGGESTED MAP OS Explorer OL13 Brecon Beacons (East)
>
> START/FINISH Grid reference: SO 386302
>
> DOG FRIENDLINESS Mostly on leads, can run on common if no sheep
>
> PARKING On east side of B4347, south of lychgate, facing south
>
> PUBLIC TOILETS None en route

Abbey Dore Court Garden stands on the site of the former Red Lion public house where, in 1837, the inaugural meeting of the Board of the Dore Union Guardians took place. It was their job to commission, construct, and manage a workhouse in the locality. The unworkable law, under which each parish was meant to cope with its own poor, had been replaced by the Poor Law Act. Thus the 'Union' was a group of 29 parishes. Another facet of the 1834 legislation was compulsory provision of schooling for workhouse children. At that time there were five workhouses within Hereford City, one of which subsequently served as part of the County Hospital. Right up until its partial demolition in 2002, the building still bore the stigma, among elderly people, of having been 'a poorhouse', raising their reluctance to be admitted to it.

Poverty Within

'Riverdale', as the Dore workhouse buildings are marked on the map today, is a remote place, well away from Abbey Dore itself, which has never been a metropolis. The most disliked rule, and perhaps the least necessary, was the one that forbade 'inmates' to leave the premises. The rules of the workhouse – in fact, taken from one in Hereford – were strict but not Draconian; criminal acts were rare. Breaches were often punished by reducing diet (but such punishment could not be given to children). The diet's key elements were bread, gruel (an inferior porridge of oatmeal and water) and potatoes. Five ounces of meat per person were allowed two days per week and one-and-a-half ounces of cheese on four days per week. Most of the residents were aged or infirm; many had additionally suffered some other misfortune: blind persons, abandoned wives, unmarried mothers, and so on; and many in the workhouse were children.

In 1929 legislation transferred responsibility for residents of poorhouses to county councils. During the Second World War the Dore workhouse was used for tractor assembly. The buildings were subsequently converted into a modest number of private dwellings, but in the height of their workhouse days they had

ABBEY DORE

accommodated between 80 and 100 men, women and children. Nevertheless, the physical conditions inside the workhouse may have been little worse than those of many agricultural workers living within its 29 parishes, who endured the discomfort of damp and cramped cottages without a solid floor.

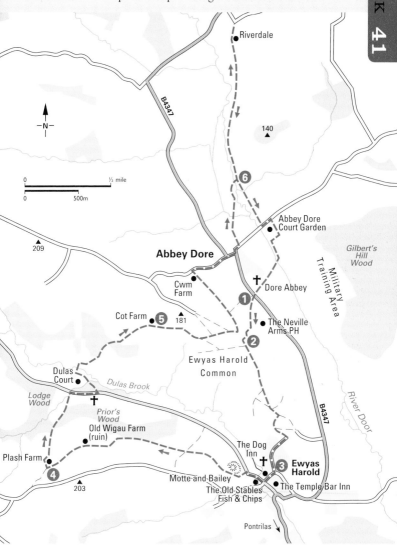

WALK 41 DIRECTIONS

1 Cross the B4347 at the lychgate. Slant to the field's top left corner. Go up through a gap near the white cottage's garden, hugging a hedge on your left to a stile. In 20yds (18m), turn right up a hedged lane to Ewyas Harold Common.

2 This is the prescribed route but dozens of paths and tracks criss-cross here. Across the immediate concrete track take the left diagonal ride. In 65yds (60m) take the slightly left option. After 45yds (41m) bear right. In 275yds (251m), when some 35yds (32m) beyond a solitary ash tree, fork

Overleaf: Dulas Brook at Dulas Court (Walk 41)

right for 40yds (37m). With trees behind you and bracken in front, turn left, soon descending slightly, for 200yds (183m) to a multiple junction. Go half left on grass (not between bracken). After 120yds (110m) turn left on a big gravel track. Just beyond a seat, fork right down a rutted track. After a cluster of three houses swing right, over a cattle grid.

3 Down in the village, turn right then right again. At the sharp bend, ascend some steps. Aim left of a spinney. After old buildings ascend three fields. A waymarker takes you briefly into trees alongside an old wire fence. As you leave the trees, swing up to a boundary corner. Keep field-edges on your right, passing near a ruin, to Plash Farm.

4 Walk through the farmyard, then get behind the farmhouse by turning right twice. Go down to the bottom corner. A sunken lane leads to a road. Turn right, then left to Dulas Court. Cross the brook by a bridge beside new buildings. Turn right in 30yds (27m), through an orchard. Go diagonally up the meadow into

WHAT TO LOOK OUT FOR
At the start, high up on the abbey side of the lychgate is a dedication to a soldier who died in the last weeks of the First World War.

conifers. Walk uphill for 40yds (37m) to a track, turn right for another 40yds (37m), then fork right, uphill, following waymarkers. Out of woodland, aim for a pole, then pass between the buildings of Cot Farm.

5 Walk with a hedge on your left. Keep this line across waymarked fields, to regain the common. In 70yds (64m) join a track (left part of the hairpin), then 70yds (64m) further, go straight ahead on a green sward, soon joining another track. Some 50yds (46m) before a house, which you should recognise from earlier, turn left. Waymarked stiles over deer fences lead to the lane by Cwm Farm. Turn right. Before Abbey Dore Court Garden find a stile at a tiny bridge. In a huge field with tall poplars at the end, find a metal gate over half-way down on the right.

6 Waymarked stiles lead to Riverdale, now a cluster of older and newer stone houses. Retrace your steps to Point **6**. Now keep on the east side of the river. Turn left at the road. In about 60yds (55m), take a well-waymarked route between the military fence and the gardens. A concrete footbridge, a meadow and an agricultural graveyard lead to the abbey.

WHILE YOU'RE THERE
Many people are drawn to this part of Herefordshire by Dore Abbey. Originally part of the great Cistercian abbey, much of it was built between 1175 and about 1220. It was restored and re-roofed as a parish church by the philanthropic Viscount Scudamore in the 1630s; he also added the tower. In Ewyas Harold, St Michael's Church is a fine building and contains a 13th- or 14th-century effigy of a lady holding her heart in her palm.

Hergest Ridge at a Trot

Rise up from a market town to a glorious ridge overlooking Wales.

DISTANCE 7.5 miles (12.1km) MINIMUM TIME 3hrs 30min

ASCENT/GRADIENT 1,115ft (340m) ▲▲▲ LEVEL OF DIFFICULTY +++

PATHS Meadows, field paths, excellent tracks, 12 stiles

LANDSCAPE Panoramas on Hergest Ridge

SUGGESTED MAP OS Explorer 201 Knighton & Presteigne

START/FINISH Grid reference: SO 295565

DOG FRIENDLINESS Sheep country and some horses

PARKING Mill Street car park (east and west sides of Crabtree Street)

PUBLIC TOILETS On Mill Street

This is not the hardest walk in this book, but the first thing you need to know is that 'Hergest' rhymes with 'hardest'. Kington was essentially a wool-trading market town, on an important drovers' route. St Mary's Church was certainly visible from afar, a tall spire on a hilltop position. The Norman tower had to be rebuilt in 1794. The remainder was built later, mostly 13th century, with Victorian additions. The suggested map shows 'Race Course (disused)' along Hergest Ridge. It was a focus of entertainment from 1825 to 1846. It had replaced the one on Bradnor Hill (north of the town), first used in the 1770s. Racing stopped round about 1880, but being up on the hill must have given considerable relief from the nauseating stench of the town's surface sewage. The Hergest Ridge section is one of several highlights for walkers undertaking the Offa's Dyke Path. The path and the ancient earthwork itself often do not coincide, but that doesn't seem to matter – they still represent a mighty piece of history and a fine long distance route. Adjacent to Bradnor Hill is Rushock Hill, and a particularly well-preserved section of the Offa's Dyke that the National Trail route follows – you will have to make a separate excursion on foot to see it.

The industrial estate that straddles the road south-west of Hergest Bridge stands on the site of a 'camp', a wartime military hospital, dilapidated parts of which remain. Closer to the town, on the opposite side of the road to the toll house, the (almost) level field once served as a landing strip – all 300yds (274m) of it!

KC3 – The Kingston Connected Community Company

A small market town on the Anglo-Welsh border seems an unlikely place for 'cutting edge' technology, which is precisely why KC3 exists at all. Founded in 1993, it was a synthesis of private and public money (Apple Computers, British Telecommunications, the Rural Development Commission and the then Department of Trade and Industry). It has shown that information technology can be applied to regenerate a declining rural economy and rejuvenate the community. The company stands on its own feet financially, and subsidises its community activities. It's located off Bridge Street.

Hergest Court

Hergest Court was once one of the many properties owned by the Vaughan family. Vaughan's wife's brother had been murdered, for which she effected revenge in dramatic fashion. Dressed as a man, she attended an archery contest where her brother's killer was, and despatched him with a fatal arrow. She then fled. Sir Thomas Vaughan was killed in the Wars of the Roses. Their alabaster effigies lie in Kington's St Mary's Church. Beside the recreation ground stands Lady Margaret Hawkins School – much changed and expanded, it's been a school since 1625.

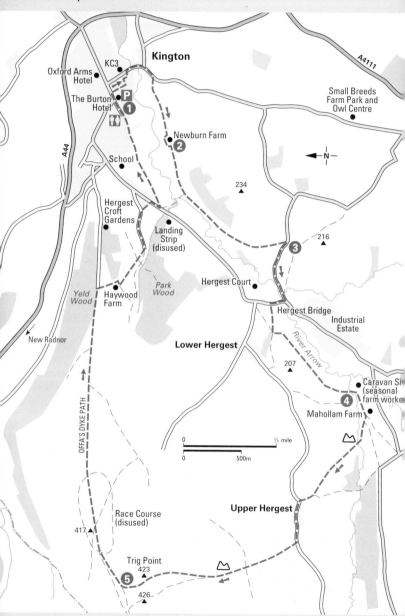

WALK 42 DIRECTIONS

1 Walk down the High Street. Take an alley on the right, between a hairdresser and a menswear shop. Zig-zag to Bridge Street. Turn right. Cross the River Arrow. Take the driveway to Newburn Farm.

2 Go round three sides, then take a gate beyond a corrugated shed and stables into a field. After an area planted with trees (including cherry and ash), when you see a footbridge, move up and left to take a stile to a right-hand field-edge, under huge oak limbs. Walk for over 0.5 mile (800m) through meadows, curving left to a stile and steps, between two houses, down to a road.

3 Turn right, then right again to cross Hergest Bridge but after 125yds (114m) take a left fingerpost. Within 100yds (91m) veer right to cross a stile into trees. Out of trees, see a stile ahead, but go beyond it to a waymarker, to cross a meadow to a line of sweet chestnuts. Over a difficult stile, turn right, along an awkward path across a steep, wooded bank. After 325yds (297m), a stile puts you into another meadow. Cross a footbridge. Contour to a gate then cross waymarked meadows using a two-plank bridge, a double-stiled footbridge and steps down to a metal footbridge.

4 At a road on a caravan site for seasonal farm workers turn right. After 40yds (37m) find a stile (perhaps overgrown), right. Almost immediately, take a second stile beside a huge, damaged oak. At a track beside Mahollam Farm bear right, downhill. Do not stay on this green lane, but go right, finding another metal footbridge. Ascend steeply, soon in farmland. Cross fields to a lane. Turn right. Go left for 325yds (297m), to a gate. Now go straight up to the '423m' trig point on Hergest Ridge, avoiding the densest gorse.

5 Keep ahead for 80yds (73m) but, on seeing a wide path cut through bracken, go a quarter right; beyond it lies a pool. Turn right. Now stride out for 1.5 miles (2.4km), ignoring an early left fork. On the road again, when 30yds (27m) beyond a sign proclaiming 'Kington – the centre for walking', turn right. Round Haywood Farm, continue down to a cattle grid; cross this. Down this road after 350yds (320m), look for a fingerpost beside the white 'No. 31'. Go down this field. Turn away from Kington for 120yds (110m), then turn sharply left, following 'Tatty Moor'. Cross meadows to the recreation ground. Join Park Avenue, which becomes Mill Street.

Harley's Mountain Air

*This bracing walk in a corner of Herefordshire
is just what the doctor ordered.*

DISTANCE 3.75 miles (6km)   **MINIMUM TIME** 2hrs

ASCENT/GRADIENT 755ft (230m) ▲▲▲   **LEVEL OF DIFFICULTY** ✦✦✦

PATHS Meadows, field paths, woodland tracks with roots, 11 stiles

LANDSCAPE Wooded hillsides and farmland, views to higher Welsh hills

SUGGESTED MAP OS Explorer 201 Knighton & Presteigne

START/FINISH Grid reference: SO 364672

DOG FRIENDLINESS Horses near Lingen but few sheep,88 exciting woods

PARKING At St Michael's Church, Lingen (tuck in well)

PUBLIC TOILETS None en route

After the Second World War, the nascent European Economic Community devised the well-intentioned Common Agricultural Policy (CAP) to address food shortages. This 'good idea' did not embrace the diversity of farming conditions, practices and cultures, and could not foresee subsequent technological advances. In its later years the CAP fell into disrepute – its supporters might say because it was so successful – because surpluses resulted, and maintaining these perishable stores was costly. The scheme was also contentious because many of the larger players in the global food market, in particular the United States, were jumping up and down, saying (correctly, it seems) that exportation of such surpluses was illegal because they arose from subsidised production.

Set Aside

It was therefore deemed necessary to reduce the European output – 'set-aside' was introduced in the 1992 CAP reforms. Under the scheme, farmers essentially left some fields 'unfarmed' and received financial compensation for loss of income. However, the scheme was completely contrary to the traditions, instincts and ethics of many in the farming community. In 2001, for example, farmers were obliged to leave 10 per cent of their food acreage out of food production. The payment (or 'compensation') received was partly dependent upon which side of the Welsh border your land lay. In England the rate was £88 per acre (£218 per hectare) but in Wales it was £77 per acre (£190 per hectare). Set-aside land could be used for growing 'industrial' as opposed to food crops. Set-aside land could be either part of a crop rotation or left for successive years. In environmental terms, favoured fields would be those adjacent to existing hedgerows, copses, commons and the like. However, in 2008 the obligatory rate was set at…0%! The abolition of obligatory set-aside is on the cards.

Single Payment Scheme

Set-aside has been superceded by the so-called 'Single Payment Scheme' (SPS) which is now the central scheme for subsidising agricultural activity throughout the European Union. The scheme has been in place since 2005, but is constantly being adjusted. Its philosophical core cuts the link between the quantity a farm produces and the size of the subsidy it receives, instead making, as the name suggests, fixed, one-off payments, and in particular rewarding environmentally friendly farming practices. Clearly the solutions to the agricultural economy will continue to tax policymakers for some years to come.

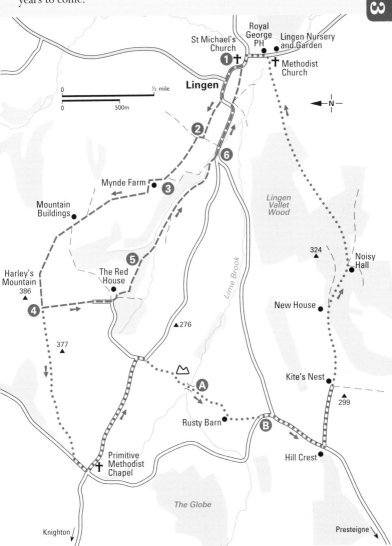

WALK 43 DIRECTIONS

① Walk away from the church and cross over to take the minor road signposted 'Willey'. When you reach the first bend, follow the fingerpost directly ahead. Beyond a difficult gate beside a small corrugated shed, walk by the right edge of this paddock and the next, reaching a little-used lane in trees.

2 Move right to strike up the field, passing an oak stump. Follow a waymarker up and slightly right. In the corner, negotiate the rusty gate between better ones. On reaching a lovely, brick-built cottage skirt right of this, and the collapsed buildings of Mynde Farm. Find a gate on the right behind a low building still standing.

3 Go down and up a wide meadow to a stile seen from afar. Veer left, passing beside Mountain Buildings on a deeply rutted, rocky track. Some 160yds (146m) further, enter a large field. Go diagonally across the field (but if ridged with potatoes, for example, follow two field-edges left); then keep that line, now with a hedge on your left. Within 200yds (183m) take a gate on the left. Two fields further along this breezy ridge reach another gate with a small pool to the right (possibly dry in high summer). Above and behind you is the dull, grey trig point. (Walk 44 leaves here.)

4 Turn left, along a (perhaps overgrown) sunken lane. Descend steadily for 650yds (594m). At the bottom move left, down to a small gate. Through trees, shortly emerge close to The Red House. Go dead ahead, finding a narrow path within trees, right of the garage and beside a hedge. Within 40yds (37m) negotiate a metal gate. Do not be tempted down; instead move left (yellow waymarker, not blue), beside a

wire fence for just a few paces, then, maintaining that fence's line, proceed to walk below a narrow ridge on a faint green tractor track for perhaps 100yds (91m). When the ground ahead drops steeply into a dell, turn half left to walk in trees beside a meadow (the field-edge is easier). In the second meadow, where the trees bulge out to the left, dive back into the woodland – a waymarker on an oak (right) is reassuring.

WHILE YOU'RE THERE

Cross into Wales and visit nearby delightful Presteigne. It is surely only the border that keeps it out of the Black & White Villages Trail. Its main street is strewn with black-and-white buildings. The Judge's Lodging in Presteigne is a hands-on illustration of life and its social strata in the 1870s.

5 Go steadily ahead, sometimes boggy, in woodland, lush pasture, then bracken for 0.5 mile (800m). At a wobbly silver-grey gate drop left 10ft (3m) to a waymarked stile into a once pollarded, streamside lane. Reach a road.

6 Turn left. After 450yds (411m), on a bend, go straight down the field to a hedge beside some farm buildings. Find a single-plank stile in that left corner. Go ahead, to another stile that gives on to the village road – take care! Turn left to the start (or go right and cross carefully, to go via the church to your car).

WHERE TO EAT AND DRINK

Lingen's pub, the Royal George, has fine ales from Wye Valley Brewery, and a beer garden. It is open lunchtimes Friday to Sunday. The tea rooms at Lingen Nursery and Garden are open from Easter to September, whereas the nursery is open from February to October; all are closed on Tuesday and Wednesday. If visiting Presteigne, you'll find several options, from 'olde worlde' pubs to cafés and little restaurants selling pizzas.

Upper Lime Brook Valley

Take this longer, upland route for extensive views into the Welsh hills.
See map and information panel for Walk 43

DISTANCE *7.5 miles (12.1km)* MINIMUM TIME *3hrs 45min*
ASCENT/GRADIENT *1,080ft (329m)* ▲▲▲ LEVEL OF DIFFICULTY +++

WALK 44 DIRECTIONS (Walk 43 option)

At Point ❹ go straight ahead, not left, for over 0.75 mile (1.2km). Crossing arable fields and pastures, descend to reach a minor road. Turn left for 120yds (110m), then left, signposted 'Lingen', soon passing the diminutive Primitive Methodist chapel of 1862. More than 0.5 mile (800m) further, turn right at a T-junction. Now in just 70yds (64m) take a fingerpost right, across a field to a stile, and down into the valley. Veer a fraction right, but don't be misled by sheep tracks – pick your way down this, at times inordinately steep, pasture, to find a gate then a double-stiled footbridge in a boggy patch to the right of some massive ash trees, Point ❹.

Scramble up a short, wooded bank to walk with a field boundary on your left for about 250yds (229m), taking a deeply rutted farm track into a miniature valley with tall trees. Here ignore an option to fork right on a track, instead swinging left, ascending, alongside an old, square-wire fence. However, in just 80yds (73m), at a fence corner, keep ahead, to pass through a gap beside a defunct stile, to the left of a rusty barn. Walk 80yds (73m) diagonally left to a working stile.

Walk up the left side of the field to a minor road, Point ❸.

Turn left, along the road, for 650yds (594m). Turn left at Hill Crest. Just past a large metal barn at Kite's Nest take a track between hedges, not into a field. When the outbuildings of New House are near your left take the lower, better-defined track, into pleasant woodland. On seeing a garden shed before Noisy Hall, fork left. Beside the house, initially keep just within the trees, on a narrow path close to pasture on your right. This goes deeper into woodland but after 600yds (549m) a stile gives on to meadows. Two fields later, go into trees again, for a gently descending track. (At a stile and gate, a large oak has grown around a gate bar.) This becomes a deeply sunken, barrel-like lane between meadows once more. This ends at a dirt track to the public road, beside the Methodist church. Turn left through the village, then the lychgate to St Michael's Church.

WHAT TO LOOK OUT FOR

In Lingen, St Michael's Church has attractive 19th-century wooden shingles on its bell-turret. On the slopes of Harley's Mountain, notice how the eroded farm track has a bed of rock, illustrating how shallow the soil is.

A Wander from Weobley

A pretty black-and-white village is the focus for this pleasant amble.

DISTANCE 5 miles (8km)   MINIMUM TIME 2hrs 15min

ASCENT/GRADIENT 164ft (50m) ▲▲▲   LEVEL OF DIFFICULTY ✦✦✦

PATHS Minor lanes, meadow paths, village streets, 19 stiles

LANDSCAPE Gentle farmland and orchards, village

SUGGESTED MAP OS Explorer 202 Leominster & Bromyard

START/FINISH Grid reference: SO 401517

DOG FRIENDLINESS Lead needed on lanes and preferred in fields

PARKING Village car park (signposted)

PUBLIC TOILETS Beside museum in Weobley, on B4230

WALK 45 DIRECTIONS

Begin by perusing the map in the car park as you may find it useful for exploring the village later. Also, you can speculate on the function of the quirky little building to your left, within the car park. Not only does it have a brick base but, above the doorway, the 'white' cladding is over yet more brickwork.

After a heavy snowfall Weobley is at its blackest-and-whitest, taking on an almost surreal, monochrome guise. At any time of the year, the village remains a delight: in the spring it's inspiring, in the summer it's beautiful, and in the autumn it's simply exquisite. Opposite the car park entrance is an exemplary medieval black-and-white property, but instead of diving into the village, turn left, then left again, towards the Church of St Peter and St Paul. It has a Norman south doorway, parts of the chancel are 13th century, and the tall tower is from the 14th century.

Walk round two sides of the church lane, then go straight ahead on a dirt track. Keep on this track at a stile by a traditional orchard. Curving right, follow the track down the right side of a huge field, then straight ahead over a stile, guided by power poles. Turn right to walk, fenced in, beside a lane. At the T-junction go right, on a tarmac lane beside a Bulmers' orchard. The prominent trees in the young hedgerow are traditional 'standards'.

After 275yds (251m), take a stile into this orchard. In perhaps 60yds (55m) is a damaged but living oak – walk just 20yds (18m) beyond this, to a waymarker on a

WHILE YOU'RE THERE

Weobley's museum is open Monday to Thursday only, and bank holidays (phone in advance). Just off route, before the Marshpools Inn, is the Lance Hattatt Design Garden. A few miles north, towards Pembridge, is Dunkertons Cider Mill (closed Sunday), and a restaurant in two 16th-century barns.

chest-high pole, obscured by two apple trees of a row. This points you diagonally left, through the orchard, then two fields bring you to a minor road. Turn right for nearly 0.75 mile (1.2km), through the hamlet called Weobley Marsh. Pass a turn for King's Pyon then, 50yds (46m) after Link Cottage, take the stile, left. Over the next stile turn right, not ahead, then cross a two-plank footbridge to walk beside New Street Stone House. Follow its driveway to a T-junction. Turn left for 100yds (91m). Turn right (or continue for 140yds/128m for the Marshpools Inn). Follow the left field boundary to another minor road. Turn right, then left at the T-junction. At the 'Give way' turn left, but in just 30yds (27m) turn right, through a strip of woodland, into Garnstone Park; very little remains of Garnstone Court. Now go 650yds (594m) along this gravel track to a gate and stile. Here take the right diagonal yellow marker (not ahead), aiming for the flakily whitewashed far end of a long, high brick wall. Turn right here on another dirt track, keeping ahead when it bends right.

At the next gate, don't go through but turn left – now, along a green motorway. Make a beeline for Weobley, heading for its church spire which is the second tallest in the county.

At a kissing gate go straight through, beside the ring and bailey. Another gate and you are at the top of the main street.

The village's name probably derives from 'Wibba's Ley', a ley being a woodland glade and the land belonging to a man with that Saxon name. It is known that glove-making and brewing were among the 7th-century activities in the village. By the time of Domesday it was known as Wibelai, later evolving to Weobley. The village claims an association with the famous Hereford cattle. James Tompkyns (or Tomkins) had 33 children, begot by (only) two women. Two of these children were early cattle enthusiasts – they obviously knew how to breed – but in truth the Herefords that we know today were not bred in a controlled way until well into the 18th century. In spite of this connection with cattle, conspicuous in its absence from Weobley today is any visible market place. The isosceles triangle at the top of the village, now occupied by a rose garden and bus shelter, marks the spot. The market hall was demolished in the mid-19th century, whereas a fire – probably started in a basement bakery – destroyed the adjoining row of 15th- to 17th-century houses in November 1943.

To return to the car park, go straight down the main street, then turn left before The Red Lion Hotel.

Overleaf: A rainbow seen from Offa's Dyke Path (Walk 46)

Cats and Dogs on the Black Hill

Visit the highest point in the two counties, where the harsh life has been portrayed in an absorbing novel.

DISTANCE 8.75 miles (14.1km)   MINIMUM TIME 4hrs

ASCENT/GRADIENT 1,475ft (450m) ▲▲▲   LEVEL OF DIFFICULTY +++

PATHS Muddy patches, stony descent, lanes, minor roads, 5 stiles

LANDSCAPE Mountainous plateau incised by green valleys

SUGGESTED MAP OS Explorer OL13 Brecon Beacons (East)

START/FINISH Grid reference: SO 288328

DOG FRIENDLINESS A good yomp, but may be sheep grazing on tops

PARKING Black Hill car park (signposted)

PUBLIC TOILETS None en route

On the western edge of Herefordshire are three valleys: the River Dore in the Golden Valley, the Escley Brook in the Escley Valley and lastly the Olchon Brook in the Olchon Valley. The Black Hill lies, sometimes literally, in the shadow of the Black Mountains that here delineate the Welsh border.

High Start

Even at the car park – almost 1,300ft (396m) – you are higher than most tops attained elsewhere in this book. Known locally as 'the Cat's Back', Black Hill distinguishes itself by being the highest peak in Herefordshire (and in Worcestershire) that the Ordnance Survey names on its maps. The Ordnance Survey gives no such attention to the actual highest point in Herefordshire, a knuckle on one of the Black Mountains' splayed-out fingers, lying as it does along the boundary with Wales – so let's call that 'the Dog's Back'. In fine, summertime weather you cannot fail to enjoy this airy walk, but should you do it in cold and wet conditions, you will need a heart of stone not to empathise with those upland farmers who have no choice but to be working outdoors in such conditions.

Realistic Fiction

Bruce Chatwin's 1983 book *On the Black Hill* was largely biographical, tracing the history of the Jones family through some 70 years of farming on the Black Hill. He had spent much time in the Herefordshire borders and had befriended several people. At first it may seem odd that a book about outdoor, farming people should be claustrophobic, but it is a short distance from solitude to isolation, and even in the 21st century people who work on the land are often in solitude for protracted periods of time. In the case of the novel's Jones brothers, Benjamin and Lewis, they are emotionally intense, largely because they have so few relationships and because of their blood ties. (In the film of the same name, directed by Andrew Grieve and released in 1988, the actors playing the brothers were real brothers too.)

Bruce Chatwin's *On the Black Hill* was his first novel. He had arrived at writing by a roundabout route, first as an auctioneer and later as head of one of London's famous auction houses, then as an archaeologist. His diverse career was typical of his life; he attributed his adaptability and somewhat 'nomadic' lifestyle to his wartime childhood, during which he was cared for by various aunts in various places. By the time he died in 1989 he had written several other novels, realising his goal of not being a formula writer but making each book quite different to any that preceded it, although many people find them 'inaccessible'.

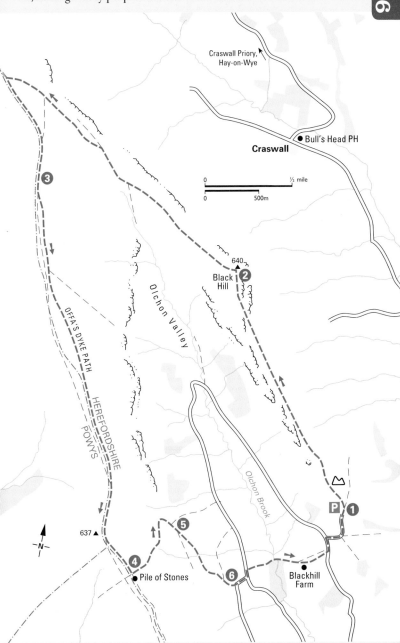

WALK 46

WALK 46 DIRECTIONS

1 From the car park cross a stile to go straight and steeply up the clear track. Enjoy the airy path, or, if the wind is strong, walk in the lee on the eastern side when the terrain permits. The gradient varies over the 1.5 miles (2.4km) to the trig point.

WHERE TO EAT AND DRINK
The menu at the Bull's Head free house, Craswall, includes pan-fried hake, Craswall pie and Olchon lamb. Dogs welcome. In Michaelchurch Escley the Bridge Inn, adjacent to the Escley Brook, offers home-cooked food using local produce. It has a brookside beer garden. Dogs and children are welcome.

2 Fork left, leaving a pond to your right. Follow what is now an easy, broad ridge for 1.75 miles (2.8km), to a low, concrete slab. Turn left here, on an initially flagged path, joining both Offa's Dyke Path and the border between England and Wales. In a little over 0.5 mile (800m) is a very indistinct top – at over 2,300ft (700m), it is the highest point of all the walks in this book.

3 Now carry on for 2.5 miles (4km) along the ridge: the point where you turn off is indicated by a pile of stones and a similar concrete slab indicating Offa's Dyke Path again – this point is approximately perpendicular to the sharp end of Black Hill. You may be able to see your car from here, and the re-ascent to return to it.

4 Turn left. The descent begins with a left-hand traverse. After 650yds (594m) be sure to swing round to the right, heading down the valley. When 140yds (128m) beyond this sharp bend, note, but do not take, a waymarker indicating a left turn option (in late summer the waymarker may be concealed by bracken). After 30yds (27m) come to a very finely forked junction.

5 Be sure to take the lower, left-hand option; do not go 'straight on', that is, the right fork. Descend to a fence. Turn right in front of a stile, cross a stream and reach a kissing gate within 50yds (46m). Some 160yds (146m) further is a kissing gate by a tree stump. Walk along a sunken track, then go down an old sunken lane. Later ignore a stile on the left and reach a minor road.

6 Turn left to descend to a junction. Turn left. Within 60yds (55m) take a footpath on the right, down into trees to cross the Olchon Brook, then re-ascend. Go round buildings at Blackhill Farm and continue up following waymarkers through trees to the road you came in on. Turn left, then right to return to your car.

WHAT TO LOOK OUT FOR
Look out for energetic Offa's Dyke Path walkers. They started in Chepstow and so are only a couple of days into the walk. Those who started in the north are probably tiring, so won't overtake you!

WHILE YOU'RE THERE
A few miles along the road to Hay-on-Wye, not signposted and tucked out of sight in a valley, are the forlorn remains of Craswall Priory. Craswall is the third and final Grandmontine priory in England, the others being in Grosmont, North Yorkshire and Alderbury, Wiltshire. The priory was probably built in the 1220s, and abandoned in 1441. It is a listed Grade II, Scheduled Ancient Monument.

Shrunken Clifford – an Original Settlement

A circuit of a 'backwater' of the River Wye, visiting a village with a significant history.

DISTANCE 5.5 miles (8.8km) MINIMUM TIME 2hrs 30min

ASCENT/GRADIENT 560ft (171m) ▲▲▲ LEVEL OF DIFFICULTY +++

PATHS Field paths and lanes, awkward embankment, over 30 stiles

LANDSCAPE Rolling hills and Wye Valley views

SUGGESTED MAP OS Explorer 201 Knighton & Presteigne

START/FINISH Grid reference: SO 251450

DOG FRIENDLINESS Lots of stiles; lots of cows, sheep and horses

PARKING Roadside parking at St Mary's Church, near Clifford

PUBLIC TOILETS None en route

Clifford itself was a planned Norman town of perhaps 200 dwellings. The parish appears as Cliford in the 1086 Domesday survey, and maps of Herefordshire dating from the 1360s show only three significant settlements – Hereford itself, Wigmore and Clifford. We know that William Fitz Osborn (later the 1st Earl of Hereford) had a castle built on the site in about 1070, having been given the ground by William the Conqueror.

Defensive Flooding

Apart from the natural defences afforded by the spur of land beside the river (the name deriving from a modest cliff near where the river was fordable), an earth dam has been identified on the western, upstream side of the castle. This would have enhanced the castle's defences by creating a considerable lake – it's a natural flood plain, as the absence of contours on the map shows. What you see today – which isn't much – was built in about 1250, but the earthworks are substantial. The castle is privately owned (sold in 2002), so you have to peep in from the road. As one of several Welsh border defences, it has at times been a focus of war, suffering particularly in the 16th century. As for the vanished parts of the castle, doubtless the stone was put to good use – it is said that both Upper Court and Lower Court in the village are built of it.

St Mary's Church

A contemporary building that has escaped the ravages of war and withstood the ravages of time is St Mary's Church. The church is in a 'Red Riding Hood' setting, a good 0.5 mile (800m) uphill from the castle; the reason for this separation is not completely clear – perhaps it was literally to distance it from conflict? Much of the present-day church is Victorian. Among its features are four family shields on the belfry roof and a rare 13th-century wooden effigy, which bears a striking resemblance to the one in Hereford Cathedral of Bishop Aquablanca. Priory Farm is so-called because it was built on the site of the priory of Cluniac monks, founded in about 1130, and named after a religious order originating in Cluny in France some 200

133

years earlier. The adjacent fish ponds, presumably dug out by the monks, would have provided their community with a valuable source of protein. On the route you'll cross and re-cross the dismantled railway that connected Dorstone, in the heart of the Golden Valley, with Hay-on-Wye. It joined the line that served Hereford and Hay (and continued on to Brecon) about a mile (1.6km) south-west of Clifford, the line from Hereford having been built 25 years earlier, in 1864.

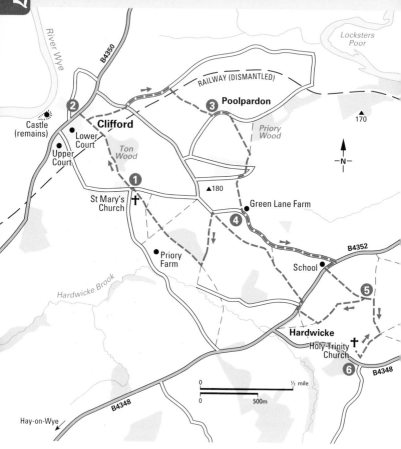

WALK 47 DIRECTIONS

❶ A few paces past the road junction at the corner of the churchyard, take some wooden steps on the right. Yellow arrows indicate your route. On leaving Ton Wood more arrows lead across the old railway towards Clifford. Leave the last meadow beside a house, noting the two arrows for those coming from Clifford.

❷ Walk to the road. Turn left then right for the castle. Retrace your steps to Point ❷. Now take the arrow pointing to a row of oaks. At the tarmac beyond follow 'Unsuitable for heavy goods vehicles'. On the right, after 440yds (402m) search for a stile up three steps. It's probably hidden by hazel (and bracken). Across this green strip scramble down, then use wooden steps to get up the railway embankment again.

Half-way up the field switch the hedge from your left to your right. Find a smart metal gate beside a derelict yellow harvester. A wooded path soon reaches a lane.

3 Turn left. In 230yds (210m), before a large, renovated stone dwelling, strike right, to a stile behind six hawthorns in a dip. Alongside a garden, take the rough track joining two tarmac lanes. Turn right for perhaps 30 paces. A waymarker points towards a stile in trees. Go straight down this field to meet a lane.

4 Turn left along the lane, admiring the cobbled courtyard of Green Lane Farm. Stride out for 0.5 mile (800m) to reach the B4352. Turn right. In 120yds (110m), cross to a stile. In this vast meadow aim to the right of trees

on the skyline, then the stile by a white-walled house.

5 Pass through the garden. Take the bridleway, right. After a leafy interlude join a stony track, soon very straight, but within 160yds (146m), where a footpath crosses, turn right. To reach Holy Trinity Church go forward over stiles to a driveway and turn right.

6 Return to Point **5**. Go diagonally left to a stile completely hidden by a protruding hedge. Turn right, around two sides of this field. In the next one turn right, along the field-edge to reach the B4352 at a footbridge and stile. Cross this to take a fingerpost seen to the right. Cross two fields; in the third keep ahead at the corner but veer one small field left to a gate (not a road gate). Aim well right of an oak to a jutting out corner. Over the stile here, aim for the gap behind the nearer solitary tree. Walk to the seen road. Recross this field diagonally to a gap, guided by the other finger on the post. Veer left to a stile. Turn right beside woodland. Soon turn right by finding a double stile in the hedgerow to contour above Priory Farm. Having skirted to the right of a house, St Mary's Church, seen across fields ahead, is easily reached.

Rent-a-Bee in the Golden Valley

A busy pilgrimage from the River Dore to the River Wye and back, across a heavenly landscape.

DISTANCE 6 miles (9.7km) **MINIMUM TIME** 3hrs

ASCENT/GRADIENT 1,165ft (355m) ▲▲▲ **LEVEL OF DIFFICULTY** +++

PATHS *Minor lanes, good tracks, meadows, couple of short but severe descents over grass, 19 stiles*

LANDSCAPE *A route with many picnic opportunities!*

SUGGESTED MAP *OS Explorer 201 Knighton & Presteigne or OL13 Brecon Beacons (East)*

START/FINISH *Grid reference: SO 313416*

DOG FRIENDLINESS *Grazing land, but some freedom in sections of woodland*

PARKING *Car park beside Dorstone Post Office*

PUBLIC TOILETS *Beside village hall, near green*

Bees are fascinating. One could write a book this size just on the biology and sociology of bees, and still have much to write. We shall have to content ourselves with a little bit about how Herefordshire has benefited from them. Beekeeping is a combination of science, art and skilled labour, an all-consuming hobby or, occasionally, a way of earning a living. After Dorstone, the next village going south is Peterchurch, home of Golden Valley Apiaries and where David Williams and his father before him have kept bees since 1959.

Contract Pollinators

At one time David and June Williams' Golden Valley Apiaries managed over 540 colonies of bees, although today the number is greatly reduced. A typical year would yield 8.5–10 tonnes of honey – about 20,000 1lb jars – but one exceptionally good year produced over 13 tonnes. The honey, which has won prizes at the Three Counties Show and the Royal Welsh Show, is largely sold through local shops, with some being sold in bulk to packing companies. (A meagre 5 per cent of the 25,000 tonnes of honey eaten in the UK each year is produced by British bees – so much for food mountains.)

All this honey has to be collected. Bees typically forage over a distance of about 1.5 miles (2.4km). Fruit growing is financially a high-risk venture – apples and pears, but more so the soft fruits such as blackcurrants, raspberries and strawberries – so rather than leave pollination to chance, growers hire colonies of bees. Although almost impossible to measure scientifically, it is generally reckoned that hiring bees during the flowering period can improve the fruit yield by 30–40 per cent compared with merely relying on the local, wild bee population.

Most of Golden Valleys Apiaries' work is within a 40-mile (64km) radius. Bees are early risers – to deliver bees to a site means getting the hives into a vehicle before first light – otherwise, particularly on warmer mornings, the bees may have taken flight. Typically the hives are kept on a site for four to six weeks. Bees don't like the rain, but yields of honey are only seriously affected if there is very protracted wet weather. The greatest danger to the flowers they are pollinating is a late frost, but the fruits themselves are also susceptible to adverse weather such as heavy downpours and freakish hailstorms at picking time.

Any species is susceptible to diseases and viruses. More than 100 colonies were lost in the Golden Valley when varroasis struck in 1994–5. Across the UK, between winter 2007 and winter 2008 the varroa mite destroyed 30 per cent of our wild bee colonies. The crab-like mite *Varroa jacobsoni* is a mere 0.04 inches (1.1mm) long and 0.11 inches (1.7mm) wide. It is a parasite, sucking blood from the bee. In addition, the mite lays eggs in the honeycomb; once hatched, these suck blood through the body wall of the pupa of the honey bee. The colony will almost certainly be lost as the mites are often found only when it is too late.

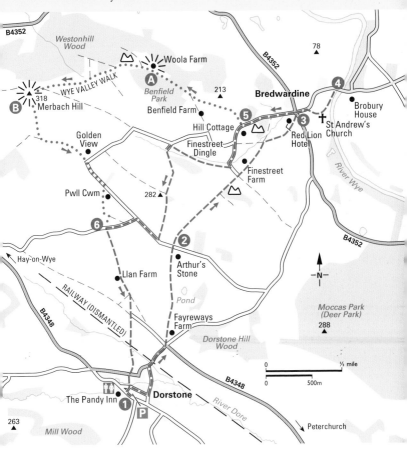

WALK 48 DIRECTIONS

❶ Go down the near side of the triangular village green but turn right (not to the church), passing

fine houses with finer views. At the lane end turn left, passing D'Or Produce Ltd (who pack potatoes). At the B4348 care is required. Go straight ahead, bridging the River

Overleaf: Arthur's Stone (Walk 48)

Dore. Be sure to switch sides before the road bends severely right. Follow the driveway towards Fayreways Farm. The farm track gives way to pastures leading directly up to Arthur's Stone.

WHILE YOU'RE THERE

St Andrew's Church at Bredwardine is very much Kilvert's church, being where the Victorian diarist was rector when he died of peritonitis in 1879. It has a huge 12th-century font. Brobury House Gardens – seen from Point ❹ – extend to 5 acres (2ha) in formal Victorian style.

❷ Beyond Arthur's Stone take a fingerpost. Cross the second field diagonally. Follow the left side of an ineffective fence to a stile left of the corner. Two fields further, descend very steeply on grass beside larches. Keep beside the hedge to find an awkward stile. Take the lane but skirt right of Finestreet Farm using several gates. In another steep meadow, find a stile below and left of a massive standing oak with a fallen one beside it. Cross a field diagonally, to pass beside a renovated, timber-framed house. Beyond is Bredwardine.

❸ Cross the road carefully. In 80yds (73m) an avenue leads to St Andrew's Church. At the very end, a stile and waymarkers lead

WHAT TO LOOK OUT FOR

On the village green in Dorstone is a simple sundial. The stone post on which it stands is reputedly the remains of a cross, the top of which was detached during Oliver Cromwell's time. Arthur's Stone itself is a chambered tomb dated 3700–2700 BC. As you begin the ascent from Bredwardine, look for alpacas in a field on your left.

to Bredwardine's bridge over the River Wye – ideal for a picnic.

❹ Go back to Point ❸. Take the '25%' gradient road beside the Red Lion Hotel. Go 700yds (640m) up this lane, including its steepest section, to just before Hill Cottage: here a fingerpost points right, and behind you is a '1 in 4' sign. (Here Walk 49 goes right.)

❺ Keep ahead, ignoring a right turn to Arthur's Stone. When the road rises sharply after a stream, find a gate on the right, just past Pystil Gwn. Now ascend this dell (Finestreet Dingle) guided by blue arrows. In front of a house, turn left then left again, to skirt a plantation. A row of hawthorns points to your stile near the brow. Pass to the right of some scrawny pines, keeping this line to a minor road. Turn right. In 325yds (297m) turn left (sign '20%'). Down here after another 325yds (297m) find a fingerpost, hidden behind a holly tree. (Walk 49 rejoins here.)

WHERE TO EAT AND DRINK

In Dorstone, The Pandy Inn, a 12th-century freehouse, overlooks the village green. It has a delightful beer garden, play equipment for children and award-winning food. Roughly half-way round, in Bredwardine, the handsome Red Lion Hotel is an irresistibly convenient place to stop, particularly as you'll pass it twice.

❻ Soon join the track visible ahead. Rattle on, to and through Llan Farm. However, 220yds (201m) beyond it, take the diagonal footpath (not the old lane, right). Cross a sunken lane, the old railway, then the village playing fields to reach the road near the church. Cross over, then skirt right of the churchyard, along a fenced path, to the village green and the start.

A Climb on to Marvellous Merbach Hill

It's worth the climb to attain the high spot dividing the valleys of the River Dore and the River Wye.

See map and information panel for Walk 48

DISTANCE *7 miles (11.3km)* **MINIMUM TIME** *3hrs 30min*

ASCENT/GRADIENT *1,330ft (405m)* ▲▲▲ **LEVEL OF DIFFICULTY** +++

WALK 49 DIRECTIONS
(Walk 48 options)

At Point ❺ on Walk 48 turn right, along a bridleway (not into a field). In perhaps 100yds (91m), where the drive bends, take a gate with a blue 'Wye Valley Walk' marker. Follow the field boundary on your left, initially staying low. Through a triply fastened gate, very gradually ease away from the field boundary, ascending. Join the track from Benfield Farm in the fourth field, 50yds (46m) before a cattle grid.

Now seemingly in forest, walk for 400yds (366m), to between the penultimate and final pole before the farm, Point ❹. A hand-painted footpath sign marks some steps up into trees, skirting Woola Farm. What price its view? Join a steep, extensively cracked concrete track, uphill.

Pass to the left of some corrugated sheds just before the brow of the hill. This is something of a false top, but the way to Merbach Hill is clear ahead. In the last field before the common, hug the field boundary on the left to observe the right of way, then, over the stile, turn right for 40yds (37m) to resume your line.

A green path cuts through scattered hawthorn, silver birch and rowan in what in summer is a sea of otherwise impenetrable bracken and brambles. You will come to a double fork (no waymarkers). Keep ahead, for here you are just 130yds (119m) from the trig point and a memorable view. Whatever the origin of the Golden Valley's name may be, when you are atop Merbach Hill you cannot refute that you have struck a rich vein of scenery.

Prominent to the south-west is Hay Bluff: head towards it for about 60yds (55m), to reach a good path. Turn left, to an easily seen wicket gate. Enjoy this modest, sheep-grazed plateau to pick up a dirt track from Golden View. Go ahead on the tarmac lane for 350yds (320m), taking a fingerpost just before Pwll Cwm. Go down the left edge of two fields. Turn left on a gravelly, grassy lane for 50yds (46m). Now take a stile on the right. Out of this field, take a few paces to your left, rejoining Walk 48 at a fingerpost and a holly tree, Point ❻.

WALK 50

The Lower Olchon Valley

Walking way-out west, where the times are scarcely a-changing.

DISTANCE 5.25miles (8.4km)   MINIMUM TIME 2hrs 45min

ASCENT/GRADIENT 655ft (200m) ▲▲▲   LEVEL OF DIFFICULTY ✦✦✦

PATHS Lanes, tracks and field paths in mixed farmland, 22 stiles

LANDSCAPE Rolling farmland and the Black Mountains ridge

SUGGESTED MAP OS Explorer OL13 Brecon Beacons (East)

START/FINISH Grid reference: SO 324287

DOG FRIENDLINESS Under close control, mall dogs may need help on stiles

PARKING About 300yds (274m) north of The Crown, Longtown, on castle road, in long bay beside row of large, new houses

PUBLIC TOILETS None en route

WALK 50 DIRECTIONS

Take a path behind the modern telephone box. Drop diagonally right across two meadows to reach a road bridge. Turn left, crossing the River Monnow, then right. Just 20yds (18m) beyond a bridge over the Escley Brook turn left. Strike diagonally right to a wooden handrail and waymarker; ascend to a track near a house. Turn left. Pass to the left of a shed with cars, then walk with field boundaries on your left. Cross a rivulet by a three-plank bridge, the Escley Brook now on your left. After stepping stones, walk through woodland. Leave by wooden steps, then a stile. Go slightly right to a gate. Continue, roughly level, with a young hedgerow on your left.

The Herefordshire Council funds various grants for regeneration and environmental improvement throughout the county. Applications may be made by small landowners, individuals, parish councils and community groups. One example is the Orchard and Hedgerow Grant scheme, for up to a maximum of £500. Grants are available for the planting of hedgerows and also for laying already established hedges, planting or pruning fruit trees for orchards, and fencing associated with any of the planting activities.

Over a new stile, dip down for some 30yds (27m) to turn right, joining the upper track, with its 'Countryside Access Scheme' noticeboard. Take the permissive path to cross five waymarked fields, enjoying views of Black Hill (Walk 46). A footbridge leads you into a small conifer plantation. Two gates lead to a minor road. Turn right. At a T-junction go left for 30yds (27m), then walk up four right-hand field-edges; fine views open up to the left.

By the end of the 1990s average income per head from farming had fallen to just below £10,000. Incomes have risen slightly since then, but 2001's foot and mouth outbreak hit Herefordshire

WALK 50

WHERE TO EAT AND DRINK

Hopes of Longtown is the proudly independent village stores and post office; here, in season, you will find locally sourced produce. The Crown has an open fireplace and offers standard fare. In Clodock is the Cornewall Arms.

hard. One possible vehicle for economic regeneration is the Herefordshire Stone Tile Project. About 7 miles (11.3km) east-north-east of Longtown is Dore Abbey (see Walk 41). Its stone tile roof underwent urgent repair, using stone from nearby quarries or delves. The plan is to reopen other local delves and train local people in the largely forgotten skills of tile dressing. In the case of Dore Abbey, much of the funding is coming from English Heritage. Hopefully this will act as a catalyst to the private home market, for many of the county's private dwellings have stone roofs. In reality, tile dressing might provide a second income for farmers and other agricultural workers – the shock and strain to the wrists of working the stone full-time would be injurious.

Cross the top field of Mynydd Ferddin and one more diagonally, to a hedged and fenced track. Follow this track for less than 150yds (137m), turning right over a stile (with a waymarker). In nearly 0.5 mile (800m), including an enormous pasture, join the lane just left of Upper Brooks Farm. After about 400yds (366m), where this bends left, take the right-hand path option, diagonally across the field, not down its left-hand side (note the overgrown fingerpost behind you!). Turn half right (there should be a hedge on your left-hand side), but in 40yds (37m)

take a gate on the left. Move to the right, to walk with the hedge on your right. Descend steadily, passing the ruinous buildings of Garn-galed to your left. Pass just to the left of a single-chimneyed house but immediately move right to a stony, rutted, sunken lane. At the 'Clodock' sign go straight across the road, beside a house. Veer right, to be beside the infant River Monnow. At the bridge turn left, then immediately right, soon entering St Clydog's churchyard (but keep on the road for the nearby Cornewall Arms).

The church is a terrific, largely Norman building. Inside you'll find a three-decker pulpit (with a clerk's stall below the vicar's stand and, at the bottom, a reading desk). Also here are three, centuries-old oak chests. The parish's money box had three different locks – the vicar and two of his churchwardens would have held one key each. Don't miss a fascinating stone tablet setting out the Hereford Assizes judgement of 1805 that established monetary payments to be made in lieu of tithe payments. The dove (a symbol of peace) carved in one corner is thought to mean that both sides were happy with the judgement.

Leave by a fenced riverside path. Cross several meadows, easing away from the water to a tarmac road. Turn right. Soon pass Tan House Farm. Shortly ignore the right fork, to pass the Old Ebenezer Chapel; your car is 0.25mile (400m) ahead.

WHILE YOU'RE THERE

Longtown Castle has just enough to fire the imagination, and stunning views. St Margaret's Church (between Longtown and Vowchurch on a minor road) has a beautiful rood screen.

Walking in Safety

All these walks are suitable for any reasonably fit person,
but less experienced walkers should try the easier walks first.
Route finding is usually straightforward, but you will find that
an Ordnance Survey map is a useful addition to the route maps
and descriptions.

RISKS

Although each walk here has been researched with a view to
minimising the risks to the walkers who follow its route, no walk in
the countryside can be considered to be completely free from risk.
Walking in the outdoors will always require a degree of common
sense and judgement to ensure that it is as safe as possible.

- Be particularly careful on cliff paths and in upland terrain,
  where the consequences of a slip can be very serious.

- Remember to check tidal conditions before walking on the
  seashore.

- Some sections of route are by, or cross, busy roads. Take care
  and remember traffic is a danger even on minor country lanes.

- Be careful around farmyard machinery and livestock, especially
  if you have children with you.

- Be aware of the consequences of changes in the weather and
  check the forecast before you set out. Carry spare clothing and
  a torch if you are walking in the winter months. Remember the
  weather can change very quickly at any time of the year, and
  in moorland and heathland areas, mist and fog can make route
  finding much harder. Don't set out in these conditions unless
  you are confident of your navigation skills in poor visibility. In
  summer remember to take account of the heat and sun; wear a
  hat and carry spare water.

- On walks away from centres of population you should carry a
  whistle and survival bag. If you do have an accident requiring the
  emergency services, make a note of your position as accurately
  as possible and dial 999.

COUNTRYSIDE CODE

- Be safe, plan ahead and follow any signs.
- Leave gates and property as you find them.
- Protect plants and animals and take your litter home.
- Keep dogs under close control.
- Consider other people.

For more information visit www.countrysideaccess.gov.uk/things_
to_know/countryside_code